# Snowed Out Atlanta

*The Inside Story of SnowedOutAtlanta, the fastest-growing Facebook group in history.*

What happened here on this page can not be overstated, and it deserves to be known about and remembered. From all over the state people reached out into cyberspace and made a difference in the lives of others. Ordinary people stayed awake all night long getting help to others, finding resources, sharing important information and giving comfort to those who just needed to know that people cared.

What Michelle Sollicito and all her fellow admins did to compile information and connect people in need with those who could help and keep up with thousand of posts and multiple pages was a major logistical effort that most people would have thought impossible.

Hours and hours and then more hours were spent by people who were consumed by the need to help, tears were shed in worry and then again in joy when people were helped. There are hundreds of stories now about how this page saved lives, that is not an exaggeration, it happened over and over again for more than 24 hours. Strangers reached out to strangers time and time again, and no one that came to this page with a plea for help went unanswered. The pace of posts here at times was more than 100 posts per minute.

Some were here for help when they had no other place to turn, some were here to offer help to everyone they could reach, some were here for support during the times they had to wait to hear from loved ones, some offered prayers, some offered compassion, some found a shoulder to cry on and a hope to hang on to.

Everyone that was here came for different reasons, but everyone who was a part of this is taking away with them something that can not even be explained. So as the jokes are made about how the south handled snow, as the political blame gets all the attention, as people move on, it's important to know what these people did. There are more stories of regular people doing amazing things than can ever be truly counted.

**Alicia Sears Hernandez, Jan 30 8:48 p.m. (A member of SnowedOutAtlanta)**

## Snowed Out Atlanta

**First Edition**

**Copyright © 2014 Michelle Sollicito**

**ISBN:** 978-1-304-95503-6

**Self-published using Lulu at** http://www.lulu.com

**Information can be found at** http://www.snowedoutatl.com

# Contents

# Acknowledgements

In writing a book like this, there are so many people to thank that I really want to just say "Thank you to everyone!" but there are a few people who stand out and really deserve some extra love.

Everyone who did the "admin" job during any time for the SnowedOutAtlanta group deserves recognition, but Yasemin Yalcinkaya went way beyond being an "Admin" on the site. As I told her many times during the whole experience, she became my best friend, my confidante, my supporter, my crutch through the tough times. She held the site together when I simply *had* to take a step back for personal reasons, and without her we would not have saved nearly so many people. She has had some health concerns since Snow Storm 2 and my thoughts are with her.

Walter Thomas Little (who also has health concerns), Jelena Crawford (ditto) and Rachel Bruce also helped tremendously. Walter has a background in the Red Cross, Ham radio and is just a general helpful guy - especially during disasters. Jelena Crawford created the awesome SnowedOutAtlanta Google Maps with *no notice* during the peak period of SnowedOutAtlanta, and helped countless people as a result and Rachel helped bring those maps to the people by enabling them to add shelters to the maps and assisting others in finding locations near to them. To all the other admins, a big "Thank you!"

So many heroes were on the SnowedOutAtlanta site that I do not feel right about picking one or two to mention here, but I think Craig Catalfu and Jason Patrick really stand out because of the sheer number of people they helped and the number of hours they were helping people for. Thank you guys!

Also to all the other groups who helped – such as 4x4's Helping Atlanta and Georgia Jeepers. Thank you!

I would like to thank my proof-readers for proof-reading my book. I could not have asked for better proof readers! I would also like to thank Linda Gunter for her sections on psychology, included in the book and to Leticia Mathis and Laura George for their contributions and help throughout SnowedOutAtlanta.

I would like to thank the many SnowedOutAtlanta members who allowed me to use their stories in this book, including Jessica Loncar, Lori Stein, Elizabeth Cervantes, Katie Norman Horne, Jason Patrick, Kelli Rochester and so many more.

I would like to thank Facebook – Mark Zuckerberg especially – as without Facebook none of this would have happened – and you can see a more detailed "thank you" to Mark at the end of the book.

Of course, in addition, I would like to thank my 50,000+ friends, all of whom helped in so many ways that this book would never be finished if I included them all!

We are Atlanta! Together We Are Awesome! Pay It Forward!

# Chapter 1 – Snow Storm 1

## The Calm Before The Storm

Something amazing happened on January 28th, 2014.

It started like any other day for me.

Getting up at 6 a.m. was tough, as it was every Tuesday, because I knew I had to get the kids to school before I could go to work. I work part-time at a consulting firm called Apogee Interactive (which works with the utility industry), in Tucker, Georgia - a good 40 minutes' drive from my house in moderate traffic. Most of the time I work from home but Tuesdays I work in the office.

Today, I really wanted to get there as early as I could because there had been an announcement that schools might close early due to snow expected in the early afternoon. I did not want to feel bad about "ducking out" of work early, given that I had been unable to do much work since Christmas because my kids had been sick so much. I wanted my kids out of the house as soon as possible; later, I was to be so glad they were inside it, safe and warm!

As I browsed Facebook that morning I saw many parents complaining about the possibility that school might be closing early that day. People were still reeling from the "Snow Day without snow" we had had a couple of weeks earlier when the schools were closed simply because low temperatures were predicted – not because snow was expected. Comments like "Only in Atlanta" and "Only 2 inches of snow are forecast, and yet they are shutting the schools early? Don't they know we have to work to earn money?" flooded my Facebook page. I was pretty angry at these comments, and felt sorry for the local School Board, as I knew how difficult such decisions were to make. I am sure later that day, many people regretted those posts!

I put my husband on alert that he might have to pick up the kids from school if it closed early because I would be too far away to get to them quickly enough. He agreed, though I think he, too, was pretty frustrated that the schools were closing early.

I headed to my car to go to work.

I really loved working with Apogee Interactive, not least because the CEO of the business (Susan Gilbert) and her husband, Joel, are the nicest bosses I have ever worked for. So much so that I had gone back to work for them a second time! I had previously worked for them shortly after arriving in America from the UK ten years earlier and had loved it then. So when Susan kept asking me to go back to work for them I found I could not resist.

I had worked in IT/EBusiness Consultancy for 25 years, but Apogee Interactive was a "repeat client." Just before I had worked for them ten years ago, I had been very involved in Disaster Recovery and Business Continuity planning in the IT field and had even written a book on the subject. So it made sense that when I worked for them 10 years ago, I had worked on a StormCentral™ demo application for

Georgia Power – I believe it was the first one of its kind. Long before mainstream use of mapping tools such as Google Maps and ARC-GIS, this application allowed a Utility to plot outage information on a map so that customers and the media could determine how many current outages there were and how long an outage would last. I had no idea that later that day my experiences with StormCentral would be so useful in helping so many people.

Looking back now, it seems a lot of my previous experiences were somehow preparing me to help people that day.

One of the things I loved best about working for Apogee Interactive is their whole ethos toward their employees: it feels like you work for a family, not a company. As I run a group called Marietta Moms and various communities supporting schools and parents in providing education to kids, working at Apogee Interactive is very compatible with my personal life: Susan makes a point of encouraging everyone to do a great deal of service work in the community. She also encourages everyone to do lots of "personal development," especially through reading business books and self-help books.

As I am already an avid reader, and am particularly interested in self-development, this is a great fit for me and at this point in time, I was just about to finish listening to "The Facebook Effect" by David Kirkpatrick[1] (via Audible.com's iPad app) on the way to work. If I had realized at the time how useful this book's contents would be to me later that day, I would have listened more carefully!

I had also been running a website for five years, with the aim of providing a new, easier, free way for "sellers" to place classified ads. The idea was to allow users to place ads using "Txts" (texts) from their cellphones, or emails from any email client (on any pc, phone or device). I had called it "Txt To Ad" and created a website at TxtToAd.com.

When I started writing my website, Facebook was not even on my radar. I used it occasionally, but put it in a similar category to "MySpace" at the time – I thought of it as a "waste of space." I would laugh to my husband about the pointlessness of some of the posts from friends, or members of the Moms group I ran, joking "I do not need to know that the moms in my mom's group changed three smelly diapers today."

But apparently, not everyone felt the same way. When I had not received an email from my best friend Michele, back in the UK, to tell me her second baby girl had arrived, and it was days after her due date, I sent her an email asking if she'd had the baby yet. She seemed quite annoyed and said "Didn't you see my announcement and pictures on Facebook?" At that point, I hadn't been on Facebook for a few weeks, so I had missed it. I was a little annoyed that she had assumed I would see it, rather than calling me to let me know her news! At that time I felt I had no daily reason to go to Facebook.

All that changed a few short months later, when Michele notified me, again, via Facebook, that she had had a "funny turn." I had known that she had not felt well since giving birth to her baby girl, but I had put that down to the fact that she had recently given birth to her second baby, coupled with being over

---

[1] The Facebook Effect: The Inside Story of the Company That Is Connecting the World by Kirkpatrick, David (Jun 26, 2012)

40. I knew I had been exhausted a couple of years earlier, when I had given birth to my second child also.

However, this "funny turn" did not sound right. She had apparently been having her haircut and when she stood up to leave she fell to the ground convulsing. It sounded like she had had a seizure.

Suddenly, I was addicted to Facebook, waiting for updates from Michele. When her update told me that the doctors at the hospital told her she had "pneumonia," I shivered. I knew pneumonia did not cause seizures. But I also knew that lung cancer *did* cause "pneumonia"-like symptoms and could also cause secondary brain tumors that could cause convulsions. I tried to ignore the panic growing in my gut. My husband was always telling me to stop making a "drama out of a crisis," and surely that was all I was doing.

But a few days later, my fears were confirmed, again via Facebook (though via a private message this time). The doctors had told Michele they suspected lung cancer and that it had spread to her brain. Although they were doing tests to be sure of their fears they made it clear to Michele, a few days before her 42nd birthday, that she was more than likely looking at a death sentence. My heart broke.

I had known Michele since we were 13 years old schoolgirls in Carlisle, in the North of England together. We had done everything together. She was so fun-loving, the social butterfly, and she was so friendly and compassionate to everyone she met. She had more friends than any other person I ever knew (real friends – not just Facebook friends!), and we had been best friends for nearly 30 years.

We had giggled about boys we liked, we had worked hard together for our exams at school, we had gone out drinking and dancing (at far too young an age!!) together. While we went on to higher education at different ends of the country, Michele came to visit me in London whenever she could and I went up to visit her in Southport (near Liverpool) a number of times while she was in college.

After graduation, she moved to London, as did a number of our friends, and Michele became the "Social Secretary" of our little group, always finding out about cheap, fun things to do in London. We went to concerts, went to see musicals, plays, movies, and went out for wonderful meals and pub crawls all over London throughout our twenties.

Together, we went on a whistle stop tour of Europe on a Kontiki bus with a group of mainly Aussies and Kiwis (Australians and New Zealanders) and had the time of our lives. That trip gave Michele the travel bug and after that she hopped all over the world at different times visiting people we had met on that trip, including visiting New Zealand, Australia, Canada and America.

Looking back, I am so glad she made those trips.

Being in America, and knowing Michele was dying made me feel so helpless. I begged her to let me visit her. She replied that I could visit her when she felt better, when she had started a treatment plan, because she felt so weak and wanted to spend time with her immediate family (her husband and the two girls). We both knew that that meant I would never see her again, but I respected her wishes. I knew that if I only had months or maybe even days left, I would want to spend as much of that time with my two children as I could.

Suddenly I understood the emotional connection so many of my friends had to Facebook. All I could do was watch Facebook feverishly for Michele's updates. She posted whenever she felt strong enough, knowing how many friends she had out there who cared about her. She posted that it was confirmed that she had stage 4 lung cancer. I tried to support and help her as much as I could. In a private message to me she was more honest about her true feelings about the diagnosis and I lost it.

On January 6th, 2011, just a few weeks after her diagnosis, Michele's husband posted a link to a song on Facebook that told me the end was near. The song by Kate Bush, entitled "This Woman's Work," tells the story of a man who is waiting in a hospital waiting room while doctors try to save his wife's life.

I could not sleep all night and kept getting up to see if there were any posts. My worst fears were confirmed when I saw a post at about 5am my time (EST) confirming that Michele had died. It felt unreal to find out that one of the most important people in my life was dead, via a post on a Facebook page. It was so surreal, I could not really accept it.

However, from that point on, I made it a point to keep up with all the people who were important to me regularly on Facebook. I decided to move my Moms group over to Facebook too. I had run "Marietta Moms" since just before my daughter was born in February 2007 but I had run it mainly on other community sites such as Meetup.com, Ning.com and Spruz.com up until now. Now I decided to move it to Facebook completely, including a "Page" and a "Group." I realized a "Group" allowed my members to discuss issues between them much better than a "Page" did, and it also gave me controls to remove any member posting nasty comments.

The more I used Facebook, the more I realized it could be a very useful tool for connecting people and helping people. I also felt it might help grow my business. So during the past year, I had integrated TxtToAd.com with Facebook, allowing people to post ads to TxtToAd.com using a Facebook group, and now I was working on integrating with Facebook in the other direction – automatically posting Antiques ads from the Atlanta area to a Facebook group called ATLAntiques, etc.

So that's why, on the way to work on January 28th, I was listening to "The Facebook Effect"[i] in an attempt to work out how to best use the social media site to promote my business. Never in my wildest dreams would I have believed that the lessons learned from that book would be used so soon, and for an entirely different purpose!

I got to the office and tried to concentrate on my work, but was instead secretly checking Facebook and the Cobb County School District (CCSD) website for any announcements about the school closings.

Suddenly I saw that schools were indeed closing early – with the elementary school my children attended releasing their students at 12:30 p.m. Panic set in immediately. Since I hadn't been able to work much since Christmas, I felt that I could not simply walk out of the office as soon as I had walked in. However, my gut told me to go home and get my kids as soon as I could, and that this snow storm would be serious.

At around 11:30 a.m. the school called to confirm that my kids were going to be picked up and I said that either I or my husband would be there. I then worked furiously to get to the point where I could leave.

I was watching Facebook closely and started to see posts reporting that snow had already started to fall in Marietta where I lived, and that traffic was already at a standstill throughout Cobb County, because so many people were leaving work and trying to pick up their kids. I called my husband to see if he had left work yet, but he hadn't.

Immediately, I worried that he would not get to the children in time to pick them up and I decided I simply had to do what I had to do. At 12:05 p.m., I told my boss I was leaving, and flew to my car.

When I first got on the road, I thought I had panicked about nothing. The traffic was moving well from LaVista Road in Tucker around to I-85, despite the first snow flurries appearing.

As I got closer to home, I realized my fears had been justified. When I started driving on the side roads, I wondered if I had made a mistake taking that route home.

My car started to slide on the ice and, despite being in first gear and tapping on the brakes, I was unable to control the car at all. I was lucky that the two times I actually fishtailed into other lanes of traffic there were no other cars in those lanes at the time, but I knew that if I was having this much trouble driving on the roads, then so were a lot of people behind me trying to get home. I could see other cars skidding out and crashing. I knew this was going to be serious immediately. I stopped the car and called my husband to find out if he had managed to get the kids from school, and was extremely relieved to hear that he had just picked them up.

Armed with the knowledge that I did not have to rush home, I slowed down to snail's pace for the rest of the journey, knowing that was the safest thing to do. I got home a little before 1 p.m. but I was traumatized by the drive I had just experienced. I knew others would be too.

I got straight on my computer and warned my colleagues at work that they should drive home immediately and that the roads were treacherous. Then I logged on to Facebook and realized that I was probably too late with my warning. There were already so many pleas from my friends and members of

Marietta Moms, trying to get information, trying to help loved ones, trying to work out which roads to take home.

One of the things I have always tried to do while running Marietta Moms is be the central source of useful information. Whenever a mom has a problem, they come to me and ask where they can get help. At first, I tried to help in this situation in a similar manner in which I had helped in past situations. In this case, that involved finding phone numbers and passing them to those who needed them, looking up traffic reports on 511ga.org, the Georgia Traffic website; contacting the CCSD (Cobb County School District) to find information on school buses that had seemingly disappeared on their routes home.

By now, Marietta Moms and friends of mine were also posting about conditions on all the various roads. We heard reports that some hills were totally impassable – everyone who tried to drive down them was crashing to the bottom.

Some of these hills, including the one on Johnson Ferry Road going down to Columns Drive, represented some pretty important thoroughfares in the metro Atlanta area. We also started to hear the first reports of 911 calls going unanswered. I again reflected on how serious the situation was.

From all the information I was getting, I quickly gathered that there were no alternative routes home: in reality, everyone was stuck. No one was getting home.

Jessica Loncar, the mother of a girl in my daughter's class, was stuck on her way home and she asked if she'd be able to come home via Lower Roswell Road. I told her no, Lower Roswell and Terrell Mill Roads -- the road she would have to take from I-75 to get to Lower Roswell -- were both like ice rinks. She wondered about other options – Powers Ferry Road perhaps? Another friend of mine told her that Powers Ferry Road was like an ice rink too. So that left only South Marietta Parkway – but I had just heard that three tractor-trailers had spun out on the exit from I-75 to South Marietta Parkway. So I had to tell her the bad news that she was probably not going to get home that night.

At first Jessica seemed understandably incredulous, unable to believe that this could be the truth. However, I later heard it took her a very long time to get home (11 hours in total) and she had to walk the last 7 miles home, which took her 6½ hours!

Here is her story in her own words:

As the news warned of the impending snow to hit Atlanta, we remained calm and knew that the snow would not hit until mid-day. Snow would be nothing—it was the ice that we should be worried about. We thought back to several years ago, when an ice storm literally shut the entire city down for three days. This would be nothing like that.

Around 9 am, we got the call that school would be dismissing two hours early, so we knew that the kids would take the bus home. My husband, Michael, was lucky enough to be working from home that day. Thus, he would be the lucky one to retrieve the children from the bus stop, which happens to be right at the end of the driveway. They only arrived 20 minutes late.

I decided I would be able to finish out my work day in Sandy Springs until 2:00 p.m. and continue to see my physical therapy patients and clients that needed my services. After my noon patient, my 1:00 patient called the office and warned to stay off the roads and get out soon. She had to turn around and return home, as cars were already sliding down her road and she had viewed some accidents already. The news stations already were discussing the terrible traffic conditions, and were warning of the impending trouble that would be in my very near future!

Still, I wasn't worried. I was only 8 miles from home, and I thought it would be an easy ride home, if not for a bit of heavy traffic. Immediately, as I got in the car at 1 pm, I knew I was in trouble. Thank goodness, I did have some snacks in my car, a car charger, and a little water handy. However, I donned only capri exercise pants and had a light jacket and scarf. I headed out on Hammond Drive, but as I turned onto Sandy Springs Circle, traffic reared its ugly head and stopped dead in its tracks. I had attempted a different route before, I saw cars in ditches and on the sides of the road already. I was stuck. I sat, and sat, and sat for over 4 hours...and traveled only a mile. 1 mile in 4 hours? I didn't know when I would ever be home. Everyone was getting out of their cars...cold...only 20 degrees...and it was definite that the bridge across the Chattahoochee River had to be shut down. No one was moving. Not at all. Finally, at 5:45 pm, I reached a safe parking lot that I could abandon my car and start a long journey. 7 miles home. I was worried about the cold, but I knew that no one could get to me, and I wasn't going to get home for a long time.

I started out, three others began the journey with me. My UGG boots gave me a bit of warmth on my feet, but they had no traction. The sidewalks were slippery, but I trudged on, updating my husband every half hour or so. The walk was slippery and slow. As I finally made it to the river on Johnson Ferry, cars were everywhere, obviously slipping and sliding all over...and in to each other. Cars abandoned. I decided to try to make it to the only store open on the route, a Kroger on Lower Roswell and Johnson Ferry. There I was able to finally use a restroom, grab a snack, rest my legs, and buy a children's hat. No adult hats were left in the store. I was freezing. The TV was on in the snack area, all deli items were gone, all staff were huddled watching the news.

I started out with no cars in sight. It had gotten dark, as it was 8 p.m. by that point, and I had my first fall as I crossed the parking lot in the sheets of ice. I trudged on. Freezing. Tired. My Nike Fitbit started "buzzing," alerting me that I had surpassed the ultimate goal of 20,000 steps in a day. Ugh. As I knew I had only a bit over 3 miles to go, I knew I could make it. Cars and groups of people became visible as I went further down Lower Roswell. Cars were stopped, and everyone was very friendly as I ran into others making the same journey. The closer to home I went, the more cars I passed. All were stopped behind stalled buses, mail trucks, and multiple cars strewn about the roads. Fall again. This time, busting my front lip. I was carrying a heavy purse, and a heavy bag with work materials that I didn't want to risk leaving in my car. Not a smart choice.

After 10:30 pm, I crossed over Lower Roswell with my neighborhood in sight. Almost breaking down. Fatigue. Frustration. But, the excitement of making it home was great. An accomplishment.

A nice teenager and her mother along the way gave me her handwarmers as her father reached her in a car. A friendly gentlemen at the senior housing community offered a coffee to me as I passed on my long walk.

My skin was bright red from the cold, and I felt I was literally thawing for hours. But I was lucky. I was able to get home. And my kids were safe.

One friend of mine, Lori Stein, was asking for help getting her husband, Eric, home. Another friend of mine, unconnected to Lori, lived close to Eric's location and was able to offer help. I acted as a go-between, relaying information about a shopping center close to where Eric was, where he could buy food, drinks and blankets. Realizing I was becoming a bottle neck to communications between people like Eric, who needed help, and my friend, who could help him, I started to think that maybe I should create a group so that people could help one another directly without having to involve me.

I later found out that Lori Stein and her husband Eric, later, in turn, helped some friends of their cousins, in the true "Pay It Forward" style that was to become so prevalent later that day, thanks to SnowedOutAtlanta.

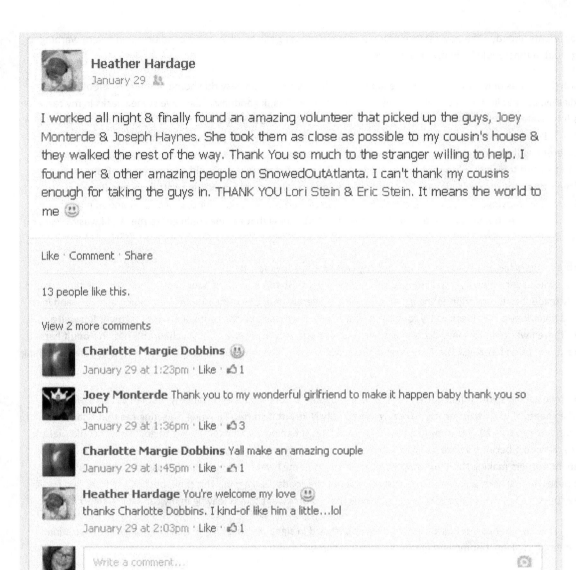

**Heather Hardage**
January 29

I worked all night & finally found an amazing volunteer that picked up the guys, Joey Monterde & Joseph Haynes. She took them as close as possible to my cousin's house & they walked the rest of the way. Thank You so much to the stranger willing to help. I found her & other amazing people on SnowedOutAtlanta. I can't thank my cousins enough for taking the guys in. THANK YOU Lori Stein & Eric Stein. It means the world to me 😊

Like · Comment · Share

13 people like this.

View 2 more comments

**Charlotte Margie Dobbins** 😃
January 29 at 1:23pm · Like · 👍 1

**Joey Monterde** Thank you to my wonderful girlfriend to make it happen baby thank you so much
January 29 at 1:36pm · Like · 👍 3

**Charlotte Margie Dobbins** Yall make an amazing couple
January 29 at 1:45pm · Like · 👍 1

**Heather Hardage** You're welcome my love 😊
thanks Charlotte Dobbins. I kind-of like him a little...lol
January 29 at 2:03pm · Like · 👍 1

Write a comment...

It suddenly dawned on me around 3 p.m. that this situation was so big, so serious, that there were a lot of people who just were not going to make it home that night.

That was when I started to call on my friends and group members to call the governor and demand that he announce a State of Emergency, in the hope that the National Guard could help the people who were about to be stranded out in the snow for the night. I posted Gov. Nathan Deal's phone number on my Facebook page just before 4 p.m. and encouraged people to call, and call they did.

I later heard via the grapevine that Governor Deal's office received so many calls and messages requesting a State of Emergency be declared that he was forced to leave a meeting where he was presenting the Mayor of Atlanta with a "Georgian of the Year" award to prepare to announce a State of Emergency. The declaration came at 5:20 p.m., about an hour and twenty minutes after my connections started to call the governor's office.

It became more and more apparent that sometimes my friends or members could help each other out better if they were in direct contact, and I was also becoming overwhelmed with being the hub, the intermediary in helping so many people, so I decided to create a Facebook group where they could all help one another directly.

I called it "SnowedOutAtlanta" because it was clear to me that so many people would be snowed out that night. I posted the link to the group and encouraged anyone who had a loved one stranded in the traffic or stuck at their offices to join it – as well as anyone who could offer help to those people. I told everyone that they could all invite whoever else they wanted to join the group, and I approved every member request. Friends invited all their friends and the group grew at an astonishing rate.

I spent most of the time at the beginning frantically searching the web for information that might help people in the group and bringing it all into one document. I then made this document the group's "Pinned Post" (this is a post on the group that "sticks" to the top of the page so that it is always the first post any member can see when they come to the group). I continually added to the "Pinned Post," finding road reports (from both official sources such as 511ga.org and unofficial sources – members of the group were posting their own road reports that seemed more accurate and up to date) indicating which roads were impassable and suggesting alternate routes. I also found the phone numbers of all the local police stations and posted Google map links to gas stations and locations where people could buy food and water.

I trawled the GEMA (Georgia Emergency Management Agency), local police and local EMA (Emergency Management Agency) websites, and others such as The Red Cross, all of which, I was surprised to find, had very few updates that were helpful.

I was already on the recipient list for many of these agencies' tweets and Facebook updates too, yet little information that came through was very useful. I flipped from TV station to TV station trying to get more up-to-date info for my members, but it soon became apparent that the most up-to-date source of information was actually coming from *inside the group* - the members of the group themselves, now that it was growing so fast.

Once I realized that the best source of current information was actually within the group, rather than on external websites, I set about asking members the questions I needed to be answered instead of searching the web – for example, where is the nearest gas station to exit 254 of I-75? And I would get immediate answers. I would post the answers where they were needed - either in response to specific questions or in the "Pinned Post" if it was general information that anyone might need.

At first there was a lot of frustration from people about delays and traffic holdups. There was anger that the Emergency Services were not helping people, and there was anger toward government officials that this situation could happen in a city as big as Atlanta.

As darkness fell, the mood turned to panic. People were starting to run out of gas, it was starting to get colder, more and more accidents were happening out on the roads and more and more people had to abandon their vehicles. Mothers were terrified for their children who had not returned home. In some cases, their school buses had seemingly disappeared on the short distance home from school. In other cases, no buses had managed to pick them up yet, and it was looking like the children would have to spend the night at school.

Eventually, we all realized we were on our own. The state and local agencies, the powers that be, were so overwhelmed with this unexpected catastrophe that they did not have time to send tweets or Facebook updates. 911 command and control centers did not even have enough manpower to answer the phones! It was scary to realize that no one was coming to the scene of an accident, no matter how severe it was. It was scary to know that no one was coming to rescue the pregnant women or the families with young children sitting in their cars. It was scary to know how few shelters were available. We could only find information on one Red Cross at one location in Sandy Springs, which was already overwhelmed, and there were rumors of a few churches opening as shelters but when people showed up at some of those churches they were closed! We suddenly realized it was up to us.

People started to realize that the only thing they could do for some people was to post life-saving tips to help them survive the night in their cars.

Elize Sanchez
-- URGENT --
As others have said, if you're running your car tonight for heat because
you will not abandon your car to find safety be sure your tail pipe remains
clear of snow and ice...

Crack the window -- just to be safe too...

Carbon Monoxide will kill you in your sleep, too.

Saying a prayer everyone is safe.

**Preston Holcomb**

Here are some tips if you do get stuck

If you do get stuck:

• Stay with your vehicle. Do not leave the vehicle to search for assistance unless help is visible within 100 yards. Disorientation and confusion come very quickly in blowing snow. Avoid traveling during winter storms. If you must travel and do become stranded, it is better to stay in the vehicle and wait for help.

• Display a trouble sign to indicate you need help. Hang a brightly colored cloth (preferably red) on the radio antenna and raise the hood (after snow stops falling).

• Occasionally run engine to keep warm. Carbon monoxide can build up inside a standing vehicle while the engine is running, even if the exhaust pipe is clear. Experience has shown that running the heater for 10 minutes every hour is enough to keep occupants warm and will reduce the risk of carbon monoxide poisoning and conserve fuel. Turn on the engine for about 10 minutes each hour (or 5 minutes every half hour). Use the heater while the engine is running. Keep the exhaust pipe clear of snow and slightly open a downwind window for ventilation.

• Leave the overhead light on when the engine is running so that you can be seen.

• Do minor exercises to keep up circulation. Clap hands and move arms and legs occasionally. Try not to stay in one position for too long.

• If more than one person is in the car, take turns sleeping. One of the first signs of hypothermia is sleepiness. If you are not awakened periodically to increase body temperature and circulation, you can freeze to death.

• Huddle together for warmth.

• Use newspapers, maps, and even the removable car mats for added insulation. Layering items will help trap more body heat.

• Keep a window that is away from the blowing wind slightly open to let in air.

• Watch for signs of frostbite and hypothermia. Severe cold can cause numbness, making you unaware of possible danger. Keep fingers and toes moving for circulation, huddle together, and drink warm broth to reduce risk of further injury.

• Drink fluids to avoid dehydration. Bulky winter clothing can cause you to sweat, but cold dry air will help the sweat evaporate, making you unaware of possible dehydration. When individuals are dehydrated, they are more susceptible to the effects of cold and heart attacks. Melt snow before using it for drinking water. Eating snow lowers your body temperature, increasing risk from hypothermia.

• Avoid overexertion. Cold weather puts an added strain on the heart.

## Elizabeth's Mom

The group grew at a furious pace after darkness fell that night. Posts were coming in at a rate of a few hundred per minute. New member requests were coming in at a rate of 300 every 15 minutes. The urgency of need was fuelling the group with both those who needed help desperately and those desperately wanting to help them. It was difficult to believe how many people were stranded, how many people were very scared, how many people were running out of gas and water.

Many of the people who were posting were ill-equipped to deal with the situation they found themselves in – they had no source of warmth in their cars – no warm clothes or blankets – and many women were wearing high heels with no other footwear available.

The "helpers" in the group were working at a frantic pace trying to assist those who were stranded, providing them with information and support. Overwhelmed by demand, many of them were waking up their friends and telling them to join the group and help out too.

By this time, many businesses were also coming to the aid of the stranded – some branches of Waffle House, Starbucks, Chick Fil A, Kroger and Publix had remained open in an attempt to help those stuck. There had been an unofficial announcement that fire stations would offer shelter to the stranded also but there was confusion about whether or not that announcement applied to *all* fire stations.

It was very difficult to know / remember which shelter locations were open and were helping people and which ones had closed down to allow their staff to go home or were not available for other reasons.

I had posted a request to ask if anyone could set up a Google Map to indicate where people could find shelter. I had created a number of Google Maps myself in the past, as part of my job, so I knew it was pretty simple to set up for someone who knew what they were doing, but I simply did not have time to do it myself that night in the midst of trying to help so many people get the resources they needed. I was, quite literally, terrified someone might die if I did not keep tabs on all the calls for help coming in.

Within a very short period of time, a woman on the site named Rachel Bruce contacted me to let me know that another woman on the site – Jelena Crawford – had created a Google Map we could use to help people find shelters and post shelter locations. I was so pleased! Rachel offered to write up some instructions on how to use the map, and as soon as she did, we made it public and posted the link in my "Pinned Post."

Immediately people started to add locations of shelters to the map – including locations of businesses such as Home Depot locations that had announced they were acting as shelters for the stranded that night.

Suddenly something else started to happen – something so incredible that it made me cry, and helped restore my faith in humanity (one of the many things that helped restore that faith that night!) - people started to offer *their own homes* as shelters.

**Shaunalynn Schonder**

I'm in Dawsonville, GA --- just a half mile from the downtown courthouse area going out on Hwy 9 towards Cumming.

If anybody is in need of a place to stay.... We have cats and kids - sleeping bags and space for sleeping - along with plenty of food!

Like · Comment · January 28 at 8:36pm · Edited

4 people like this.

**Shaunalynn Schonder**
January 28 at 8:45pm · Like

**Shaunalynn Schonder** The house is a mess... but hey - it's warm! And we have hot showers and plenty of blankets.
January 28 at 8:52pm · Like · 2

Write a comment...

## Paula Mangum

I'm on ▮▮▮▮▮▮ Smyrna/Vinings, between Atlanta Rd and Spring Rd. I have: sleep space, food, coffee, bathroom, and friendly cat. Msg me here if you are within walking distance and need a spot.

Like · Comment · January 28 at 9:44pm · Edited

It was almost impossible to believe at first – people were offering beds in their home to complete strangers, to whoever happened to show up at the door in need of rest and shelter. I quickly added my home to the list in the hope of encouraging others. And once the first few had offered their homes, offers spread like a virus throughout the group, and the shelters map soon had literally hundreds of homes spread throughout the Atlanta area.

Then I noticed another trend – people offering to pay for hotel rooms for complete strangers! Again, I cried – at the generosity of strangers towards strangers – and at the knowledge that there were people out there who cared so much that they would help in this way.

Again, this was almost impossible to believe at first, but again it set a trend to be followed by many. It was very humbling to be the person who started a group that ended up consisting of members who were so amazing and incredible.

**Autumn Martin Page**

If you are able to find a hotel room but can't afford to pay for the night, please inbox me and I will help.

Unlike · Comment · January 29 at 3:48am near Fire Island, NY

👍 You, Nadine Gasparian Bishop, Ronika Brooks, Chyron Volinski and 136 others like this.

💬 2 shares

**David N Tiffany Edmonds** God bless you
January 29 at 3:48am · Like · 👍 1

**Liz De Joseph** U r so sweet!!
January 29 at 3:51am · Like

**Danielle Smith-Bertrand** May God richly bless you and your family.
January 29 at 3:51am · Like · 👍 3

**Marcia Hacker Sutton** Better then the hotels that are charging for the night!
January 29 at 3:52am · Like · 👍 1

**Brittney McCall** Bump
January 29 at 4:01am · Like

**Rogernette Hunt** I second that. I can pay for a couple of rooms
January 29 at 4:02am · Like · 👍 10

**Princess Taryn** PSA...Target, Home Depot, Whole Foods, Kroger, Publix, and my house (Cumming/Forsyth Co) are all open to ppl who need somewhere warm to go....pass this along!!!!
January 29 at 4:07am · Like · 👍 2

**Autumn Martin Page** Just booked a room for someone in Newnan (15 miles from Peachtree City) at the Quality Inn. 2 people in the room and there is an extra double bed in the room and plenty of floor space. They said 4 more can fit.
January 29 at 4:15am · Edited · Like · 👍 33

**Jane Betty** BUMP
January 29 at 4:35am · Like

**Rogernette Hunt** I haven't gotten any responses about hotel. If you get another contact, let me know and I'll take care of the next one
Autumn Martin Page
January 29 at 5:10am · Like · 👍 9

**Autumn Martin Page** ^
January 29 at 5:13am · Like

**Christina Vo** You are all so sweet. 😊
January 29 at 5:19am · Like · 👍 1

**Hope Garrett** I'll pay for someone a safe place to stay just send me a message also.

At 9:17 p.m. that night, my friend Elizabeth Cervantes posted what was seemingly a fairly typical post at around that time on the site:

Any ideas of anything I can do to help my mother trapped on the side of Old Alabama just north of Holcomb Bridge Road in Roswell? She is 71 years old and cannot walk on ice so she cannot get out of the car to walk anywhere. She has been in the car for 8 hours straight now and is only a few miles from home. We have been on hold for AAA for over an hour, tried every tow truck in the book - none available, the police won't help, 511 is busy over and over again.

However, for me, this was no typical post: Elizabeth was my friend, someone I had known since our sons were babies together. In fact, Elizabeth had looked after my son when I went to the hospital to give birth to my daughter. I had met Elizabeth's mother on a number of occasions too. This was now personal.

I wanted to be sure Elizabeth got the help she needed for her mom. I repeatedly "liked" the post and comments in response to her post and also commented on the post to try to push it to the top of the page so that more people saw it (the technical term for this is "bumping the post").

Many people in the group had already realized that by "bumping" posts, those posts got the most attention. It had very quickly become the de facto method within the SnowedOutAtlanta group of alerting others to the posts of those who were most in need.

Because of the "bumping," Elizabeth's post got a great deal of attention – by the end of the night, there were 154 comments and Elizabeth had received numerous phone calls, "txt" messages and "Private Messages" (private messages are messages sent from one Facebook member to another which no one else can see) from members of SnowedOutAtlanta trying to help.

Elizabeth would later sum up the "surreal" feeling of this whole experience when she wrote to me:

The whole experience was somewhat surreal as so many people offered advice and assistance. I felt so helpless sitting in my warm home with my family all safe and around me and my mom out there in harm's way and me feeling completely helpless – no way to get to her. As people started offering to go to her, I worried that I would be the cause of someone else being trapped or hurt. It was a harrowing night and one I hope that none of us have to experience again, but it certainly caused me to have more faith in humanity and the goodness of people – not just the ones I talked to, but as the days went by all the stories I learned about of true acts of heroism and kindness all over the state.

Elizabeth's post at first attracted a lot of messages of support but not much practical help.

**Meg Braskett**
January 28 at 9:18pm · Like

**Meg Braskett** Is that person close?? ^^
January 28 at 9:18pm · Like

**Elizabeth Fairchild Cervantes** No, unfortunately - and she is handicapped, so it is not like she can walk anywhere. Just don't know what to do. I finally cried to the Roswell police and told her she IS having a medical emergency because she is freezing to death and they say they will send someone, but that could still be HOURS.
January 28 at 9:20pm · Unlike · 👍2

**Meg Braskett** ☹ I will be praying
January 28 at 9:21pm · Like · 👍2

**Patti Driskill Hayton** I will be praying as well!!!
January 28 at 9:21pm · Like · 👍1

**Michelle Sollicito** Holcomb Bridge Rd people - THIS IS IMPORTANT!! PLEASE HELP - she is a dear friend of mine
January 28 at 9:21pm · Like · 👍3

**Meg Braskett** Keep checking this page too for posts lots of people are being added so someone may be near!!
January 28 at 9:21pm · Like · 👍2

Then, people started posting comments offering practical suggestions and information – some trying to establish Elizabeth's mom's exact location, others suggesting businesses nearby which might be able to help and other alternatives, such as fire stations.

**Kathryn Offer Mattuch** My sister-in-law is near the intersection of Mansell and Holcomb Bridge. She says traffic has stopped moving, so she is planning on spending the night at the Racetrac gas station. This is just unbelievable.
January 28 at 9:24pm · Like · 👍 4

 **Elizabeth Fairchild Cervantes** Thanks Elli and everyone - she is in remarkably good spirits and is not actually freezing to death at this point, but she is almost totally out of gas and I am really freaking out.
January 28 at 9:25pm · Like

 **Stephanie Chambers** Bump. Praying for her!
January 28 at 9:27pm · Like

 **Sarah Darville** How close is she to Publix? They're sheltering people. I'm close, but don't know how to get her here. 🙁
January 28 at 9:27pm · Unlike · 👍 1

 **Michele Danner Byers** Perhaps if other people stranded in traffic are walking by her car she could ask for assistance to get to at least a warm gas station. People seem to be being so kind right now.
January 28 at 9:29pm · Unlike · 👍 2

 **Katie Evans** There is Publix across Holcomb bridge from where she is.
January 28 at 9:29pm · Unlike · 👍 2

 **Lori Smith** There is a fire station at 1601 Holcomb BR rd, very close to old Alabama, trying to find a phone number for you
January 28 at 9:29pm · Unlike · 👍 3

It was very frustrating to know that my friend's mom was out there at a time when I was successfully helping so many other people, but there seemed to be no way to assist her. Other people in need were at least able to leave their cars and get to a gas station, a Kroger, a Chick Fil A, or even the home of someone who could take them in.

Because Elizabeth's mom was unable to walk on the ice it seemed there was no way to help her until the emergency services arrived, and there was no telling how soon that would happen given all the other stories we were hearing on the site of people who were getting no response from emergency services despite being trapped in their cars after having accidents.

Then, the incredible magic of SnowedOutAtlanta started to surface again – some amazing members offered to walk to Elizabeth's mom's car and help her out in various ways! Given the treacherous conditions that night, such offers made me extremely emotional, very very grateful and at the same time, immensely proud of the group.

 **Victoria Louise Menzies Bennett** I might be able to walk out and take her in...if the roads are iced over.
January 28 at 9:55pm · Unlike · 👍 23

**Elizabeth Fairchild Cervantes** It is not far at all to the Waffle House or the Starbucks - assuming either is actually open. The problem is that she is unsteady on her feet on a good day (after a hip replacement on one side and a broken hip on eth other) and so cannot risk walking AT ALL unassisted in snow and ice.
January 28 at 9:55pm · Like · 👍 1

 **Victoria Louise Menzies Bennett** I might be able to walk out and take her in...if the roads are iced over.
January 28 at 9:55pm · Unlike · 👍 23

 **April Grissom** if someone could call that waffle house i'm sure someone there will be willing to go out and get her.
January 28 at 9:57pm · Like · 👍 9

 **Michele Danner Byers** Elizabeth maybe you can call those locations and explain your situation and a couple of strong men would be able to get her.
January 28 at 9:58pm · Like · 👍 1

 **Michelle Sollicito** Elizabeth Fairchild Cervantes let us know if she finds safety
January 28 at 9:59pm · Like · 👍 5

 **Victoria Louise Menzies Bennett** I only live a few blocks from the bike park you're talking about. Is it feasible to go out and look for her? You said she's in an orange honda element, right?
January 28 at 10:01pm · Like · 👍 14

 **Terri Whitley Rigby** Bump
January 28 at 10:05pm · Like · 👍 2

 **Peggy Attaway** OK, someone just posted on this page that Home Depot is offering shelter...She is REALLY close to a home depot also..very close... its just down the road she's on... as in 1/4 mile...I know she cant walk it but I wonder if she could drive down it.
January 28 at 10:05pm · Like · 👍 3

We were all overcome with emotion that these compassionate women would put themselves at risk in the cold, icy conditions and go out to find Elizabeth's mom. We were overjoyed when we heard they had found her and were sitting with her in her car drinking hot cocoa with her, having given her blankets and food!

 **Elizabeth Fairchild Cervantes** 🔵 Victoria Louise Menzies Bennett is sitting with her in the car. Suzanne is on her way to her with blankets and hot chocolate. I just got off the phone with the police and they are going to try and get to her sooner than later but it could still be hours.
January 28 at 10:50pm · Unlike · 👍 62

It really was no mean feat for someone to go out and help someone that night. It was an extremely dangerous environment to go out into. It was not simply that it was terribly cold and the sidewalks were extremely slippery. Cars were sliding right off of the roads on to sidewalks – and some impatient drivers were driving on sidewalks because they were unable to get past cars that were stuck any other way. In fact, the next day, we heard on SnowedOutAtlanta, of a young girl who was helping push a car off of the road very close to my house, who was hit by a sliding car and lost her leg.

Of course these people helping Elizabeth's mom were, by far, not the only ones to go to so much trouble to help others that night. There were countless stories of people who helped in similar ways. At first, I tried to keep track of how many people were assisted by our site, but by around 11 p.m. the count went well over 400 people, and I simply lost count. I could no longer be personally involved in every story because the stories came in at such a fast rate.

There were so many people who went out in the snow that night to offer blankets, food and drink, that it made miracles seem commonplace. So many people drove to rescue those in distress, putting themselves in serious danger, that I did not get the chance to thank many of them.

Lifelong friendships were made that night between complete strangers. People do not easily forget the person who saved their lives. No one was asking the color, sexuality or religion of any of the people they were helping, they were simply aiding fellow human beings.

Estelle 'Ivory CoastsBeauty' Kpakpo
This is my testimony.
The guy on the picture is name is William, I never met him but thanks to this Amazing group we are now friends... I wrote Tuesday night here that my twin sister (the one on the left picture) was stucked on 285 with no gas... he responded Wednesday around 5 and went to pick up my sister to take her to the shelter. He sent checked to see if she got home, I said yes. He offered to come get us and go retrieve her car. He came this morning, paid for gas to put in her car, jumped start her car and followed us to make sure the car was fine. He is one of the many Angels of this group. Thank you again William, you are now our brother 😊.

I got this message from LaTasha Ursin who was helped out that night by many "Angels," some from SnowedOutAtlanta:

OK, I finally made it home. I left work at 2:30pm and just came home at 11:10. It took me that long to make it home in the snow storm. By the grace of God, he sent Angels to help me along the way. These Angels came in different forms. They were Parkinstain Indians who help me to navigate my car, it was a young Caucasian college student who help to give me a push on my car to help me gain momentum, it was a two pair duo that put a belt on the bottom of my car and pulled me over the black ice when I could not make it, it was a young woman who went from car to car and offered her open home to those who were stranded like me, and it was even a pair of youth who offered me chips and a slim jim beef jerky when I was hungry. My God these strangers did so much for me and did not even know me that their kindness truly restored my faith in humanity. You see no matter what faith, religion, creed, sexual orientation, and/or national origin we are all neighbors. This is what neighbors should do for each other - HELP. I needed help tonight and my neighbors were my angels. I thank God for them and those who have helped me along my journey. This would also include you.

Take care and God Bless,

Tasha


The human spirit was overflowing that night and it was sometimes emotionally overwhelming to read so many stories happening live on the website, especially the ones in which people were in serious need of help – because, at the time, we had no idea if these stories would end happily or not.

So that we didn't waste time on stories where people had already been helped and were safe, members started to mark stories "Resolved."

**Caroline Gilmer Lanier**
\*\*RESOLVED\*\* My husband is stranded off of the 285 ramp (northbound) on Peachtree industrial Blvd. (On the left shoulder blocked in by several cars). His heater isn't working well and he's running low on gas. Anyone nearby with shelter/food?

Like · Comment · January 28 at 10:50pm near Roswell, GA · Edited

👍 4 people like this.

📄 1 share

**Dede Lee** I may not be too far if he can get past them
January 28 at 10:58pm · Like · 👍1

**MzNyqte Foster** Im off Peachtree ind 141 inbox me
January 28 at 10:58pm · Like · 👍2

**Leslie Garbs Wanner** Home Depot off Tilly Mill should be taking people in. If not, I'm not far.
January 28 at 10:59pm · Like · 👍1

**MzNyqte Foster** Is he near Brandsmart
January 28 at 11:00pm · Like · 👍2

**Jennifer Davis Lecaros** We are very close with a room!
January 28 at 11:00pm · Unlike · 👍6

**Jennifer Davis Lecaros** Could possibly pick him up depending on road conditions.
January 28 at 11:02pm · Like · 👍3

**Tiffany Counts** I'm about 5 miles away. I never thought that would be "too far to help." 🙁
January 28 at 11:05pm · Like

**MzNyqte Foster** ▭ im 5 mins away
January 28 at 11:06pm · Like

**Caroline Gilmer Lanier** Thank you Jennifer. I just sent you a private message.
January 28 at 11:07pm · Like · 👍1

**Kelli Persons** I have a spare bed a few exits up Peachtree Industrial if all else fails.
January 28 at 11:10pm · Like

**Caroline Gilmer Lanier** Patrick made it to a Waffle House! Thank you everyone for all your help and suggestions!
January 29 at 1:01am · Like · 👍13

It was not just SnowedOutAtlanta members who helped people that night, of course. In so many cases, companies came to the rescue of people by providing warmth, food or shelter to those who were stranded. SnowedOutAtlanta members made sure those in need knew where the nearest companies offering help were located, of course, so we worked alongside these companies all night. Of particular note were Home Depot and Chick Fil A. Home Depot went a step beyond helping people, providing heaters, beds/chairs, food and drink at almost all its locations.

It was very clear to all of us on the site that night that the companies who helped the stranded would be assured a great amount of future business for their efforts, because they received the best PR possible –

many desperate men and women posted emotional thank you messages to these companies for 50,000 people to see.  Here is one of the most compelling messages about a company offering help to the stranded that night:

Kristie Bartlett

To the AMAZING front desk staff at the Fairfield Inn/Hammond Drive: Anissa & Derek. Saying THANK YOU just doesn't seem enough. I don't know that i have ever seen such giving, selfless employees who cared so much for their guests, even those on the floor in the lobby. Not only were they kind to all of us in the lobby, giving me phone charger, mattress pad to use as blanket, but here's a story that needs to be on the news. Hotel checked in a couple where the guy had just been released from St Joe Hospital after heart surgery. They couldn't make it home & checked into hotel. Called down to front desk as man needed medication & wanted to see where they could fill it. Nothing open. Derek called over to St Joe to speak with staff about this patient needing medication to see if they would send a shuttle or something to get him the meds. They refused. At 3:00am, we all watched as Derek left the hotel on foot and WALKED a mile and a half each way to go get the medication from the hospital for this hotel guest. I was speechless.... We all will be writing to the president of Marriott about these 2 wonderful people. I'm going to post this on my timeline hoping it will be shared & will make its way to some Fairfield Inn/Marriott executives.

Like · Share · January 29 at 7:48pm near Marietta, GA

Anissa and Derek clearly went, quite literally, the extra mile, to help people, and as a result, I am sure they will be assured business for a long time to come. A number of hotels went above and beyond that night and likewise, received the best publicity that money can't buy!

 **Hope Burns** Comfort Inn on Cobb Parkway put rollaway beds in the conference room for my brother & other stranded motorists!! *APPLAUSE*. (Took my brother 8 1/2 hours to travel 13 miles before he stopped there)
January 30 at 9:38am · Like · 👍24

Other companies also received accolades on the site.  In particular, Zaxby's on Lower Roswell Road holds a dear place in my heart for the way they helped the children from my kids' school that night by taking them in and feeding them for free.

 **Chris Stokes Jacobs** Zaxby's on Lower Roswell in Marietta for donating food to the students and teachers trapped in nearby schools.
January 30 at 10:32am · Like · 👍9

**Antoinette Dempsey**

Now that we have gotten through most (prayerfully all) of the emergencies, I wonder if it is possible to compile a listing of businesses that went "above and beyond" to help stranded motorists? I think we should all be patronizing businesses that care about customers and not just the bottom line. Let's send their profits through the roof!

Like · Comment · January 30 at 8:04am

👍 Jason Lumberjack Johnson, Tish Imstillstanding Hammonds, Judy Kuniansky and 596 others like this.

🔁 14 shares

💬 View previous comments                                    50 of 5:

**Christina W Farr** racetrac
January 30 at 8:17am · Like · 👍 15

**Kim Waid LeGrand** Johnny's Pizza on Towne Lake in Woodstock took in the kids off the buses and gave them free pizza and drinks until parents could get to them.
January 30 at 8:23am · Like · 👍 49

**Vicki Harrington Franch** Home Depot donated sand, gravel, gas cans and other things to the Atlanta Police Department, and sheltered people.
January 30 at 8:24am · Like · 👍 29

**Wanda Jacobs Rogers** I know chick fil a helped out in several locations.
January 30 at 8:24am · Like · 👍 15

It was not just multi-million dollar corporations who were applauded that night. Small business owners were also hailed for their self-sacrifice..

**Cindy Willard Yun** Metro Irrigation, Inc. on Arnold Mill Rd. in Woodstock. I was with my 9 year old daughter trying to pick my 12 year old son up from school when I wrecked into the ditch in front of this business. John, it's his business, drove us 4 hours to get my son! He then went out to help 100 more people! If it wasn't for him, I would have never gotten to my son.
January 30 at 10:16am · Like · 👍 19

For a short time, SnowedOutAtlanta became a "ThankFest" site!

**Babs DeGraw Goodwyn** Super Target on Holcomb Bridge Rd let a group of disabled adults and a Just People staff person sleep in their store when their bus couldn't get them back home. So thankful.
January 30 at 8:29am · Like · 👍 22

 **Lynn Kuhn Lobis** Would love to share your post..awesome
January 30 at 8:30am · Like · 👍 3

 **Hannah Ferrell** All waffle houses remained open! Pray for those people. Some have been stuck for 48 hours, especially those employees who rely on Marta!
January 30 at 8:31am · Like · 👍 16

 **Rob Williams** Also, I'd like the rank and file employees of local school systems to be afforded a modicum of respect for their heroic efforts...
January 30 at 8:32am · Like · 👍 29

 **Charlene Anthony-Fields** Yes Rob!!! They definitely deserve it...and the school bus drivers that were stuck out on the roads with them as well
January 30 at 8:35am · Like · 👍 25

 **Sara Russell** Kroger, home depot, chick fil a, publix, amc, stars n strikes, and I'm sure many others
January 30 at 8:37am · Like · 👍 12

 **Rachel Huff Julian** Zaxby's on Old Milton in Alpharetta. They were closed and walking out the door when they got a call from a special needs school that had twenty kids with autism stuck without food or parents. They turned everything back on and made food for these kids, thereby getting themselves stuck.
January 30 at 8:38am · Like · 👍 69

 **Rob Williams** Yes, absolutely the bus drivers.
January 30 at 8:41am · Like · 👍 9

 **Stefanie Huffman** Sams Club. After the store manager didn't know how to process an order that I was trying to make, online and over-the-phone, for a box of diapers for a woman's babies, I called the 1-800-# on the back of my card, and explained the story that I was an h... See More
January 30 at 8:41am · Like · 👍 25

 **Tish Imstillstanding Hammonds** The CVS on S. Marietta Pkwy & Reynolds Rd. Allowed ppl to come inside and get warm, a lot of folk's just parked their cars and sat in them, they held my briefcase for me while I went out to help ppl get up the hill at the light, they let ppl come in and charge their phones, use their restrooms until the pipes burst and most of all they allowed those who couldn't get home to shelter their.
January 30 at 10:56am · Like · 👍 4

On the other hand, those who turned away desperate people that night will, I am sure, suffer the consequences. Many people on the site made calls to boycott such businesses in the future and there were even Facebook groups created that night just to highlight those businesses that had turned people away during the snowstorm. Of course, many of those situations may have been complicated – the employees sometimes closed businesses so that they themselves could go help others who were stranded or so that they could go help their children or elderly relatives, so none of them will be shamed publicly here.

I spent some time trying to confirm a rumor on the site that these companies were simply *not allowed* to throw people out in the cold weather during a "State of Emergency" and eventually I got confirmation that this was indeed the case:

**Michelle Sollicito**

Confirmed by a 911 dispatcher in Henry County:
TO ALL THAT DON'T KNOW The entire state of Georgia is in a STATE OF EMERGENCY This means that if someone is inside, it is ILLEGAL for that place to kick that person out, just because. If you, or someone you know has been, or is being, threatened with being "thrown out" DO NOT listen to them!!!!! Tell them to go ahead and call the police......when and if the police show up, as long as the person is not causing a disturbance and/or trouble, the police WILL NOT make them leave!!!!!!!!

Like · Comment · January 29 at 4:27am

My efforts showed me that very few people know what a "State of Emergency" declaration actually means, especially those who run companies!   I am working on trying to get that issue addressed so that people know what to do in a State of Emergency.

However, it should be noted that by far the vast majority of people that night did not need to know that it was illegal to throw people out on the streets in that situation.  I believe in "karma" – I believe that just as those who did good that night will be rewarded in some unknown way for what they did, those who did wrong that night will suffer for it without my help, and I made that clear many times on the site that night.  In fact "karma" had become the group's way of either thanking or punishing someone that night.

**⊘ Doriano Paisano Carta**

Thanks to Michelle Sollicito and everyone who's gone out of their way to help others. Remember what goes around comes around. Karma rocks.

Victoria, the woman who helped Elizabeth's mom will surely be one of those with very good karma for some time to come.  Twenty minutes after she found Elizabeth's mom, the police still could not find her.

**Elizabeth Fairchild Cervantes** The police just called me - they cannot find her but hopefully they will now that I talked them through where she is again.
January 28 at 11:10pm · Like · 👍 9

Eventually, the ambulance arrived and took her mom home.

**Elizabeth Fairchild Cervantes** Suzanne Balsley just PM'd me to say that ambulance is there now and is taking her home. Hallelujah!
January 28 at 11:24pm · Like · 👍73

As I read this post, at 11:30 p.m., I checked how many people were now members of SnowedOutAtlanta – the total was 29,000 and it was still growing at a rate of 300 members every 15 minutes.

I could not believe how many people had been helped. I had to ask people to stop saying "Thank you" at one point because there were so many "Thank yous" coming in that the people who needed help had to trawl through a huge number of "Thank yous" before they could get to the posts that could help them. It was easy for us, warm in our homes on our computers, to forget that those in real need had only cellphones, often with low battery life, upon which to seek help, and we needed to reduce the bandwidth as much as we possibly could.

But the calls for help were still coming in at a frantic rate: I was spending a lot of my time simply approving membership requests (it was not possible to approve more than about 30 requests at a time because Facebook was going so slowly at this point due to the sheer size of my group). I started looking for solutions to the rapid growth problem. I started to create sub-groups for different locations within the Atlanta area, and I encouraged members to join them.

Just as these sub-groups started to take off, Facebook contacted me to tell me they were having trouble coping with the size and growth of my main group.

## Countless Stories

From around 11 p.m. until around 3 a.m., literally hundreds of posts/comments were coming in every minute, telling the stories of people desperate for help and of those who were going out to save them.

So many stories that night involved very vulnerable people, saved lives and actions that bordered on the miraculous, it's difficult to pick out a few and highlight only those. It is important to remember that one of the strengths of the group was psychological – for many of those who needed assistance, it helped them so much just knowing that there were 50,000 people out there doing everything they could to help.

Being alone in the dark, in the cold, especially being out of food and water and having no bathrooms was extremely difficult. People suffered terribly just trying to get home. Here is one story in the words of a SnowedOutAtlanta member (Lauren):

Lauren Irish Ruske McAuliffe

I went to work on Tuesday morning in Woodstock after dropping my daughter off at her school in Acworth. I am a busy bee at work and don't concern myself with much except work. So I didn't notice everyone freaking out about the weather. At 12, my boss told me I needed to go home. I said why, it's just snow, I'm from Michigan, I can handle some dust. He said I didn't understand how bad it was and should go home. A co-worker told me I needed to pick up my kid because they are letting out early from school. Pssshh!!! This is silly. I called the school and even said I was irritated with all this hullabaloo!!! But, I saw they wanted me to go home, so I left. I got in my 1984 el camino and started my journey. As soon as I reached the entrance to the parking lot I was scared. My car slides and drifts on dry days so I knew this would be bad. I immediately called my dad and told him to pray and if he didn't hear from me in an hour then to come looking for me on bells ferry. He said to be careful and keep it in low gear. I said no problem. I just passed Hwy 92 and was drifting down the first hill after the light and got stuck. Too many cars around me and I had to honk my horn to tell people not to come near me b/c I would slide right into them. This was at 1:15. After an hour of yelling at people to get away from my car so I could try to continue to drift/whip it down and then up the hill: I had to give up. There was no more gas in my heavy ass V8. Susan, that's my car's name, could not take anymore abuse. I had already been crying. I just started balling and sobbing all over the place as I sat hopeless in my little truck. I felt like the worst mom in the world. I failed to get to my little girl. I prayed God would tell her how much I love her and to keep us all from dying too soon. I called the school half a dozen times but the lines were too busy. I tried to call my dad but the cell towers were overloaded. I called 911 and they said no help can come unless someone was injured. I got out of my car and looked around. Some cars were making it up the hill so I asked for a ride down the road. They all sped past me or just said no. I cringed at the thought of walking the 5-6 miles to her school. I could already feel my knee throbbing from the exposure to the cold. I tore my ACL two years ago and it hasn't been right since. But damn it, I wanted to hug my little girl. So I buttoned up, put my head down and started my trek. I'm a strong woman. I have been through worse. Anything is possible for my daughter. She needs me. As I walked I called the school, then her cell phone, posted on my Facebook that I needed a ride. Called anyone who would answer. But everyone was stuck somewhere or didn't have a vehicle that would do much better. I was wearing a dress so after about an hour I could not feel my knees and there roundabouts. I had to keep walking. I could feel her strength pulling each leg up and forward. Soon, the left leg felt like dead weight. I came to the first intersection and was nearly struck by a car who thought I walked too slow. And then a different car from another direction almost swiped me off the road. All I could hear in my head was how I failed as a mom. Finally my daughter answered her phone. I told her if her bus showed up then to get on it. It will take her to grandpa's house. As I choked back tears and sobs to sound brave and calm for her I could hear a bit of panic and worry in her voice. I bite down on my hand then drew in a deep breath, swallowed hard and in my nicest voice said: I love you, baby girl, I will see you soon. I am coming for you. Don't worry about me, I'm okay. I got a ride to somewhere warm and am only worried about you. She said okay, I love you too. 2 miles down the road I made it to the QT gas station. I walked inside barely able to hold back the tears. I trudged to the bathroom and slowly took off my coat and then pulled my tights down to check on my knees. They looked like someone rubbed blood all over my skin. And they felt like half thawed meat. I knew it was frost bite. I saw it when I lived in MI when kids were too poor for gloves or coats. I turned the faucet on and waited for it warm up. While I waited I rubbed my legs and tried to massage some of the frost out of them. Some hot wet towels to cover them with and massaging the muscle helped but I couldn't feel my knees still. And no matter how much heat I applied they still felt like ice. I cried harder. Too much fear was gripping me like a knife to my throat. What the hell am I gonna do. Walk, woman!! Don't go back outside, stay here and drink coffee. You will warm up soon.  I was broken at this point.  And then something happened. The school answered the phone. They said the busses can't get to the school and the kids will be staying over night. And then a friend walked into the gas station. He looked weathered and worn from walking further than I had. But, he was not beaten. I told him what happened and he said something I will never forget. "Red, you have to accept the things you cannot change and have courage to change the things you can." I say that prayer every morning and every night but sometimes the situation has to be just right for it to finally hit you like a brick.

He said, we could walk to his house, which was very close and I could stay there with him and his wife until conditions improved. I said okay but I will be moving slow b/c of the frost bite. He said not to worry b/c God is taking care of us. A few feet down the road and a stranger, in a 4x4 w/atv's, gave us a ride the rest of the way. The next day the national guard took my only daughter home to my dad's house. Two days after that whole mess started I got that hug from her.

I am walking a little funny on my left leg, and some of my skin is peeled off. But, nothing is unbearable when you know that God provides all kinds of miracles as long as you don't stop believing right before the miracle happens.

For those who had cellphones to keep in touch with our group while they went through this crisis, the group became a lifeline.

In some cases, that lifeline was mainly psychological because we were unable to physically help those people.

All we could do was to provide them with options – such as hotels, gas stations, and offers of beds for the night if they could make it to our homes.

One case that particularly pulled at my heartstrings – at all our heartstrings - was the case of a woman with Stage 4 cancer who was stranded and in desperate need of her cancer meds.

Her sister Paula's pleas for help were met with lots of information and attempts to help, but no one was physically able to get to her.  She was eventually lucky enough to be able to get an ambulance to her sister (so many who tried to call 911 that night could not get through, let alone get an ambulance, even if they needed one!)

**Paula Canant**

My sister is off hwy 41 just off 285, stranded. The only hotel is full. She is stage 4 cancer and needs her meds. She was headed back from the cancer center in Newnan at 12:00. She has been on the road for more than 7 hours. Could someone help me!!

Unlike · Comment · January 28 at 9:05pm

You and 12 others like this.

27 shares

 **Meg Braskett** If she can get to the hotel they should allow her To stay in the lobby
January 28 at 9:05pm · Like · 👍 4

 **Michelle Sollicito** Paula Canant - can she call police? See top pinned post for other options
January 28 at 9:06pm · Like · 👍 1

 **Eric G Reid** Please - Please - Help Paula - she is a blessing to so many we need to be sure her family is protected by saints and angles
January 28 at 9:07pm · Like · 👍 3

 **Shaunalynn Schonder** Not in your area, but I can send out well wishes and hugs!
January 28 at 9:07pm · Like · 👍 2

 **Layla Earls** Police or ambulance!
January 28 at 9:08pm · Like · 👍 2

 **Jacqueline Poplin Escott** Praying!
January 28 at 9:12pm · Like · 👍 1

 **Jen Wells** I would call 911. There are several hotels nearby...the galleria...the one in front of Cumberland...She may be better off going into a restaurant and calling for help from there.
January 28 at 9:14pm · Like · 👍 1

 **Katie Leatherwood** Cassandra Brownjust posted that she lives in that area.
January 28 at 9:21pm · Like · 👍 1

**Stephanie Chambers** Bump. Praying for her
January 28 at 9:23pm · Like · 👍 2

**Nina Parker** Just talked to my friends who are .5 mile from there, Paula. They are getting on this page and looking into it. 😊
January 28 at 10:10pm · Like · 👍5

 **Paula Canant** Thanks guys. She is in desperate need of her meds. It is to cold to sleep in the car even with it running. I am trying to get her to call am ambulane to get her to Wendy Hill hospital
January 28 at 11:20pm · Like · 👍3

 **Cassandra Brown** They are running I can eat them make sure she gets safe. My husband just walked the distance and said it was freezing
January 28 at 11:22pm · Like

 **Jen Wells** She's better off calling 911 and informing them of where she is so that they can get to her at some point. She needs to let someone know her exact whereabouts...IF she calls them, they may be able to direct her to a nearby church, etc.
January 28 at 11:25pm · Like

 **Paula Canant** She is at a gas station close to the hampton inn and a Waffle House. She is in a white Older model Navigator. She is afraid to get the car back on the road
January 28 at 11:26pm · Like

 **Jen Wells** IS there a way to get to the Hampton inn? Are they letting people sleep in their lobby? Or just get in to the Waffle house to be warm and safe from the cold.
January 28 at 11:27pm · Like

 **Stephanie Rogers** Paula, maybe you could call the Hampton Inn near where she is and tell them the situation. Perhaps someone there could help coordinate her rescue to bring her to the hotel.
January 28 at 11:30pm · Like · 👍2

 **Paula Canant** I finally talked her into calling an ambulane. She needs medical attention.
January 28 at 11:32pm · Like · 👍3

 **Jen Wells** So glad Paula...let us know what happens. Will be praying for her safety and well being. She will be okay, I just believe it!
January 28 at 11:36pm · Like · 👍1

 **Stephanie Rogers** Paula, so glad you got her to call an ambulance!!! Sending prayers!
January 28 at 11:39pm · Like

 **Paula Canant** I will... Thanks so very much for your support!
January 28 at 11:43pm · Like · 👍4

 **Stephanie Rogers** I'm watching ABC Channel 2 news right now. There are SO many people still out on the roads. People are in gas stations trying to stay warm. Stores that are supposed to be open 24 hours are saying they are out of food. If anyone out there has the abilit... See More
January 28 at 11:57pm · Like

 **Ellen Kucsera Collazo** Holy moly Jen! Glad you made it home safe.
January 29 at 12:43am · Like

 **Paula Canant** Thank you all for all your prayers for my sister last night!!!!!! An ambulance finally made it to her and got her to Kennestone Hospital where she is safe and got her meds.
January 29 at 9:43am · Like · 👍11

So many stories like this gave emotional support to so many people, including this anonymous poster:

> so many. I read the stories on SnowedoutAtlanta, it gave me strength, made me cry, I knew we all were not alone in this but were surrounded by angels, all those kind souls who gave selflessly to strangers. Thank you to all who helped me, I will never know your names. My faith in humanity was restored these last few days and I will now know, when we are all stuck in our day to day normal commutes, (and grumble we will) that we live in a city crowded with beautiful and generous souls!

Posts like this one received hundreds of responses (572 comments from concerned members) and that meant a lot to those seeking help:

**Amanda Zoey Hendrix**
My dad has a heart condition, feels faint, going on 11 hours and almost no food today. He thinks he may be have chest pain and he doesn't have his medication. How can I get him help???

Like · Comment · January 29 at 12:46am

Angela P. Moore-Thorpe, Chyron Volinski and 66 others like this.

28 shares

**Billy Young** What area?
January 29 at 12:47am · Like

**Amesha Mason** Where is he?
January 29 at 12:48am · Like

**Lee Coker** You or he will have to call 911 ... and it might take a while.
☹
January 29 at 12:48am · Like

**Elizabeth Rose Cole** Might be pointless but has he tried 911?
January 29 at 12:48am · Like

**Lee Coker** But do it NOW
January 29 at 12:48am · Like

**Faylene Worley** you should call the local police and let them know that
January 29 at 12:48am · Like · 👍1

**Suzanne Santana** Post his location
January 29 at 12:48am · Like

**Callen Burton** Tell him to go to the nearest place for shelter to use a phone to call u or to call 911
January 29 at 12:49am · Like

**Lynae Sammons** Chew two Asprin if he has it and call 911 where is he at?
January 29 at 12:49am · Edited · Like · 👍4

**Stacia Kartsonis** 911 is giving priority to people like him...he needs to call
January 29 at 12:49am · Like · 👍9

This one ended happily with Amanda's dad safe at a hospital nearly four hours later.

In other cases, one of our members was physically able to get help to those in need. From simple offers of food and drink to those nearby:

**Joe Schmitz**

Hey folks. I'm a trucker stuck on I-285 at exit 60 (Riverdale RD). I have some food and water for anyone close to me. I'll walk up to a mile or so to help if needed. I don't have a ton but I have enough to spare to quite a few folks. If you're pregnant, have kids with you or elderly. You will be priority. Don't be afraid to ask. Times like this-we help each other.

Like · Comment · January 29 at 7:15am near College Park, GA

👍 Amy Williams, Charlene Siemen, Julie Branch and 4,014 others like this.

📑 669 shares

**To extremely selfless, courageous acts to help people in desperate need:**

**Rebecca Watters**
I wish I could tag these amazing strangers.

I walked down to Veterans Memorial Highway to bring food and water to stranded motorists.

We found a woman and her quadriplegic husband that were stuck in her car all night. They had no food or water and couldn't walk because he is wheelchair bound.

These amazing men used their own chains on the woman's car. They helped the couple navigate to a complete stranger's house so that they could get in from the cold. The stranger opened their doors to this woman and her handicapped husband.

Gestures like this should restore everyone's faith in humanity.

Like · Comment · January 29 at 1:59pm

👍 Amy Williams, Jason Schoellen, Maria Curtis and 3,904 others like this.

Jason Patrick was one of SnowedOutAtlanta's members who went to extremes to help those stranded. The following story details just *one* of his many rescues that night.

**Tee Milli** shared Beth Galvin FOX 5's status.
STORM HERO: Brandi Underwood, 8 mo pregnant, was stranded alone for 14 hours on Langford Parkway overnight without food, water or blankets. Jason Patrick, a roofer from Bonaire, GA, was on vacation visiting the GA State Capitol. Staying with friends last night, he read Underwood's plea for help on #snowedoutatlanta and rescued her. About 8-9 truckers used their toolboxes to create stairs to help Brandi climb over the 7-foot concrete median onto Patrick's hood. God Bless these guys.

I kept coming across stories of people he helped. I lost count of how many people he saved but I know it was well over twenty!

**Joanna Hart Giles**
The fire department moved my dads truck off the road and he locked it up and a super nice person has come with a 4 wheel drive truck to take my dad home, thank you so much to a guy named Jason Patrick, a complete stranger going out of his way to help my dad and bring him home, we're so grateful!
Like · Comment · January 29 at 2:07am near Marietta, GA · Edited

I am still not sure which one of our many heroes helped in this case – the posts were all deleted from the site after the situation was resolved – but this one tugged at the heartstrings of everyone on the site because it involved a heavily pregnant woman and her young child stuck down a ravine with no food and water for hours after they crashed off the side of the road. Numerous people in the group attempted to locate her but could not:

Alicia Hicks
8.5 mths
pregnant
With a 2yr old
16 hours
stranded
In a Ravine
10 calls to 911

Many on SnowedOutAtlanta tried to help Alicia. In the end, one of our heroes (not sure who) helped the EMS find her and an ambulance rescued her. Alicia posted this picture of herself shortly after rescue - after 16 hours, stranded in a ravine with her 2 year old. Here is her story in her own words:

My daughter and I were stuck in a ravine off of Butner Rd due to sliding on ice. I had my 2 year old daughter, Charley, who had to urinate in her car seat 5 times because we could not get out of the car due to cold weather and me being 8 months pregnant, I didn't want to slip on ice. It was dark because there was no electricity for street lights. I was terrified. I called 911 10 times due to them continuing to send people for me and them turning around because they could not find us. I flashed my lights and honked my horn to no answer for my calls of help. I felt like the girl in Titanic stranded in the ocean with the whistle and no one could hear her. After they would leave, I would call again and say they missed me...they didn't come down far enough. I began to have contractions, called 911 again and they transferred me to contact Grady. The ambulance came and turned around. I called right back and said "Help, they turned around, they can't see me." I continued to honk and flashed my lights after 16 + hours in the freezing cold and they finally came walking down the hill. I cried when they arrived. Hugged them and they grabbed my daughter as she was crying as well. They finally found us. Got to the ambulance, I had very low blood pressure, glucose levels were poor, and dehydrated. Reason being, I saved all the water, fruit, and snacks for my daughter because I didn't know how long we would be stranded. Yes, I put her before me. The EMTs gave me a banana and water immediately out of her own lunch box and entertained my daughter and told me to lay down and rest.

Alicia is very grateful to SnowedOutAtlanta:

 The site was so useful and so many people reached out yet no one could get me bc of no 4 wheel drive.

---

Many other heroes went above and beyond, including this one..

**Rashan Lawhorne**

Let me share my ATL Hero of the Year Story. Brian Shroyer has a beautiful soul. He lives in my neighborhood and I have never met him. He saw me in on the road slipping crashing and sliding and pulled up beside me in his Toyota Truck. I was in a panic to pick up my 4 and 2 year old from KinderCare. Without hesitation he took me to go get them. It took us 4 hours to drive 8 miles to and from the school to get us home safe. No complaints, wouldn't accept Gas from me and didn't even think twice about helping a total stranger. Story gets better.... The very next morning after my wife was stranded out there 22 hours I texted him to let her know she was still out there. I told him where she was stranded and again without hesitation and braving the ice on the roads he went and got her and also a few other ladies getting them all home safely. I Salute you Brian Shroyer you a true Hero to us.

And, of course, the now famous Craig Catalfu who saved Katie Norman Horne, the 8-month pregnant woman who had a three year old in the car, deserves an extra special mention!

Here he posted that he was available to help anyone who needed it...

**Craig Catalfu**

Anyone in the Smyrna area stuck or need a ride let me know... Especially if walking!

Like · Comment · Share · 12 hours ago

👍 20 people like this.

🔄 3 shares

These responses came in, telling Craig about Katie

**Wendy Lockman** Craig pregnant woman at child at 285/75
11 hours ago · Like · 👍 2

 **Craig Catalfu** K on my way that direction... Where at exactly?
What r they driving?
11 hours ago · Like · 👍 1

They were referring to this post from Katie herself on SnowedOutAtlanta.

 ⊘ Katie Norman Horne
I'm almost under the 285 overpass on 75 north past the galleria. I'm 8
months pregnant and have my 3 yr old with me. We've been in the car
for over 12 hours. We are fine on gas but is anyone near on the road and
might happen to have any food or some water?
Unlike · Comment · January 29 at 1:41am near Vinings, GA

The conversation on that post went back and forth for some time, with various people making calls to
Katie and then calling Craig to communicate her whereabouts, including offers of food and shelter.

 **Michelle Sollicito** Come to my house if you can get here
http://www.ebarster.com/michellesollicito/directions.htm
January 29 at 2:01am · Like · 👍 3

 **Robert MrSmith Flournoy** It's a walk but I'm near the Galleria I can
meet her and lead her here if possible
January 29 at 2:01am · Like · 👍 9

 **Brittany Barreto** Damn I couldn't make it 20 min w out a bathroom at
8 mo lol you can get to my house if you get off at windy hill but jts
about 10 min off from there. Would be happy to have you! Hang in there!
January 29 at 2:06am · Like · 👍 9

Katie was in good spirits despite her circumstances.

 **Katie Norman Horne** Thank you for all the shares, prayers, and
positive thoughts! We are on 75 north, approaching the 285 overpass
and are at a standstill. Not panicked, just hungry and thirsty after 13
hours. Have plenty of gas.
January 29 at 2:04am · Like · 👍 15

As happened many times that night, calls to the National Guard emergency number ended in
frustration:

 **Katie Norman Horne** I called the national guard number and they
transferred me because I'm not sandy springs, dub woody, or johns
creek...every time they transfer me, I get disconnected.
January 29 at 2:26am · Like

**Katie Norman Horne**

I'm almost under the 285 overpass on 75 north past the galleria. I'm 8 months pregnant and have my 3 yr old with me. We've been in the car for over 12 hours. We are fine on gas but is anyone near on the road ar might happen to have any food or some water?

Unlike · Comment · January 29 at 1:41am near Vinings, GA

👍 You, Tanya Ariesgirl, Robin Moody, Kimberly ChefKimihou Houston and 136 others like this.

📋 108 shares

💬 View previous comments                                              50 of 594

 **Andrea Young Lakin** Just texted with her. Thank you so much! The national guard couldn't get to her, but YOU could! And DID!!!!! You are my hero:)
January 29 at 4:30am · Like · 👍 15

 **Bekah Weideman** Wooooooo hooowooooo!!! YAY YAY YAY~
January 29 at 4:31am · Like

 **Maryann Day** God Bless you Craig Catalfu
January 29 at 4:32am · Like · 👍 5

 **Kevin Pollock** Bump
January 29 at 4:32am · Like

 **Bekah Weideman** BUMP
January 29 at 4:33am · Like

 **Kelly Shelton Evans** Hallelujah! Been up all night worried about this mom and two babies. Craig Catalfu you really are an angel among us!
January 29 at 4:38am · Like · 👍 7

 **Kevin Pollock** Bump
January 29 at 4:41am · Like

 **Jennifer McKenna** No need to bump this one any longer. She has been helped
January 29 at 4:42am · Like · 👍 2

 **Mary Margaret** Amazing
January 29 at 4:50am · Like

 **Brandy Jamie Brown** What a great story with a great ending! It restores my faith in people. The world is not so bad:) Praying for all that are stranded tonight!
January 29 at 4:50am · Like · 👍 7

 **Michelle Sollicito** So glad this one ended happily - can someone tell Katie to contact me via email when she is ready as there are people who wanna do a story on her and my groups michelle.sollicito@yahoo.com
January 29 at 4:55am · Like · 👍 11

He already seemed to be a hero to all of us on the site, but later we found out that Craig had been even more of a hero than we had imagined – he himself had had already been out for hours helping push cars of people stuck in front of his girlfriend during her nightmare journey home that day. When he went to bed, he was unable to sleep knowing that people out there were still stuck in the snow.  This was Craig's post just *before* he went to bed Tuesday night, hence *before* he got up again to help Katie!

**Craig Catalfu**
January 29

Just now getting home and thawed out from going down to Atlanta Rd. and I-285 and pushing vehicle after vehicle up a slight incline! And when I say slight incline... I mean no more then 10-15 degrees of incline! Haha Ridiculous if you ask me, but I was venturing out to look for Hannah Schott who was in the traffic behind all these people that kept getting stuck! And might I add she was in this traffic for 8 and 1/2 hours already! So my mission was to find her and come home!! So... Once I got to I-285/or you could call it the terribly steep hill right before I-285... I parked my car and figured I'd walk out and help these 4 good Samaritans push cars, trucks, you name it, to help keep the traffic moving up this terribly steep hill (Sarcasm), until Hannah was next in line. And after 2 hours of pushing there she was! I hopped in and away we went with no problem making the steep steep hill! Moral to the story, Mother Nature don't let it snow in Georgia again! Hannah left work at 1:30 pm this afternoon and she got home at 11:30pm...10 hrs in the car, heck that's equivalent to driving to Pennsylvania! Crazy... Glad we are both home safe and sound! Sorry for the long post, but had to share!

*After* he brought Hannah home, and *after* trying to sleep for 15 minutes he woke up his girlfriend to tell her he had to go out and help some of those people.  That is when he found out about Katie.

**Hannah Schott** Might I add that Craig Catalfu woke me up at 1:00 this morning to tell me "There are thousands of people stranded on the roads, I HAVE to go help them!" Four hours later and he is just getting home. Ladies and gentlemen, I don't know many men like him; I am so blessed to have him in my life and this world is lucky that men like him exist. Thank you, babe...I don't know what I would do without you (and not just during the Atlantaclysm).
Yesterday at 5:20am · Like · 🖒 16

Not only that, we later found out that he helped *still more* people *after* he helped Katie!  This is Katie's story..

At the time of the storm I was 8 months pregnant and I had a 3 1/2 year old son. My office is by an exit past the airport.

I live in Marietta and I normally have 35-40 minute commute. My son is at daycare where I work. That fateful day, we received a message that they were going to shut down early around 12:30.

I picked up my son and we got on 85N. It took us 3 hours to get to Cobb Galleria and then 75N was at a standstill.

 I was texting people from work who were ahead of me and they mentioned that 6 trucks turned over so we wouldn't be moving for a while.

A couple of hours actually became 11 hours parked at the same spot. And we were not prepared. No food. Nothing to drink.

This was bad being pregnant and having a young toddler in the car. He was an angel. We played games and played with my phone.

During all this, I was in contact with my husband. He made it home but there was no way for him to get to us. He jumped on FB and a friend of ours DJ recommended the SnowedOutAltanta page. I got the link and joined the page. I wasn't worried about gas so I posted our location and that we were looking for a snack and water. I was concerned however, as I had some Braxton Hicks labor pains.

I was very dehydrated. People immediately started responding. It was amazing. My husband noticed that "Craig Catalsu" kept popping up in Smyrna helping people near where we were. I connected with him via SnowedOutAtlanta and my friend DJ posted a google map location of where I was so he could find me. Craig managed to pull close to where we were and walked to my car.

I couldn't even maneuver to the berm so he helped get us off 75 to Windy Hill. He instructed us to follow him. He's from Michigan and is very familiar with how to drive in icy situations. Slipping and sliding we got through Windy Hill and my husband met us. He had jokingly told me that it wasn't a problem. Just follow Craig and if you hit anything, we have insurance.

Actually, I never felt unsafe and I saw people helping people. It was wonderful.

Honestly, if it wasn't for Michelle and the Facebook page she created, I would have never found Craig. Craig and I were texting the next day and I found out that after he helped me, he went back out to help more people. He was truly a wonderful human being.

The next day, I also got a call from the Nightly News. Craig came over and they interviewed us. They wanted to learn about what had happened, the Facebook page that made it possible and Michelle who made it happen and helped so many people.

And, although Craig was amazing, he was not the only one who helped all the way through Tuesday night as well as well after Tuesday night was over.  Heroes were still out helping people all day the whole of the next day (Wednesday,  January 29th) until late at night - including Alan K Avery, who became a talking point within the group for his efforts to help people throughout Tuesday night/Wednesday, and *still* offered to buy food and drinks late on Wednesday for anyone he had not been able to help:

**Alan K. Avery**

Okay my new SOA friends... the sun has set... and my vehicle will no longer be able to get out... If you know of folks... that are not near me... I am happy to help with $ donations for their shelter or food. Email me here on FB. I will need to know specifics.. where and what the need is.. a number and location for the hotel or place that can give them food... otherwise... I am retiring... and getting some sleep... It's been a long day and fading .... You are all incredible and you give me hope... I am inspired.. and feel 💙. I hope one day to meet everyone of you!

Like · Comment · January 29 at 7:17pm · Edited

👍 Tish Imstillstanding Hammonds, Amy Williams, Sheri Carter Carbone and 751 others like this.

 15 shares

 **Paree Ann** I was not one of those unfortunate souls who were stranded in this, but I have seen your face pop up all day on here as you have been doing so much to help them...and I simply want to say "Thank You!" For being such a caring, giving, and special person. You have made such a difference in peoples' lives today, and you definitely do deserve some rest!
You ROCK 😊
January 29 at 7:22pm · Like · 👍 55

 **Karen Iocovozzi Jones** Thank you Alan
January 29 at 7:27pm · Like · 👍 3

 **Steven Landy** Great job Alan! Get some much needed rest!
January 29 at 7:29pm · Like · 👍 5

 **Alan K. Avery** 💙 Shirey...but .. will wait an hour or so... just in case.. You have all been incredible.. of course especially Michelle.. Thank you for allowing me to be a part of your lives and your incredible efforts..
January 29 at 7:29pm · Like · 👍 12

 **Lynnette Christina Williams** Thank you!
January 29 at 7:29pm · Like · 👍 2

 **Cheryl Lynn Ferguson-Palmer** Alan, you are a Blessing!! United we all stand, take care!!
January 29 at 7:31pm · Like · 👍 5

 **Francine Thompson** Alan, you are a true spirit with a huge heart! Thank you so much for your kindness.
January 29 at 7:33pm · Like · 👍 5

All these actions were taken during treacherous road conditions that were almost impossible to drive in even for police who had chains on their car tires.

**Eric Ax** ✔ Gina Howell Bedard Marietta Police said it gridlock at 285/75 and there police vehicles are having trouble even with chains.
January 29 at 3:07am · Unlike · 👍 2

People continued to go above and beyond into the late hours of Wednesday night helping mothers stranded with young children.

 🖉 **Jennifer McCann**
I am at a hotel off Fulton Industrial Pkwy. I am trying to get to AL so I need to continue W on I20. I only have a little car and I have a 4 year old and baby. I'm running out of formula and so I need to leave in the morning. Is it still really blocked at Six Flags Pkwy? Everything I look at shows it is backed up a lot and I don't want to leave the hotel just to get stranded on the road. I looked at the other groups but I am not familiar with the area on Atlanta. Coming from FL. Thank you!

Like · Comment · January 29 at 7:01pm

👍 Dragana Ceca Zulfic and 36 others like this.

📷 2 shares

💬 View previous comments                                    99 of 196

 **Calibabe Alltheway** I was stuck in it and if not for the generosity of the people on this page I would be sleeping in my car another night. It's the least I can do to help anyone else that needs it. Please be safe.
January 29 at 8:43pm · Like · 👍 10

 **Noni Juice** I'm not too far from Fulton Ind.... inbox me your address and a list of what u need.
January 29 at 9:07pm · Like · 👍 4

 **Jessica Ward** My grandpa stayed 18 hours around Six Flags Pkwy...just got home this morning. It's a hill that is tough to get up with all the ice. I saw salt trucks on the DOT cam but not sure if the area is completely resolved. If you must come through there, please be careful
January 29 at 9:09pm · Like · 👍 1

**Alan Lamb** Jennifer, do you know the address of the Days Inn ur staying in?
January 29 at 9:16pm · Like · 👍1

 **Ellen Kucsera Collazo** Stay at the hotel Jennifer. With the young children you are better off. Someone on here will come get you.
January 29 at 9:18pm · Like · 👍2

 **Alison Williams Pinsley** Does the hotel you are in have a store?
January 29 at 9:19pm · Like

 **Gloria Harris Jordan** The Hotels in that area are really just motel like property, so not pantries or gift shops like the Hilton or Marriott. Just an FYI, there is a Quicktrip off of Exit 46 B, Six Flags Drive.
January 29 at 9:29pm · Like

 **Alan Lamb** Been to the only one I know of here on Fulton Industrial Blvd and the lady at the desk doesn't have you listed as a guest
January 29 at 9:32pm · Like

 **Calibabe Alltheway** Please tell us when you have connected with Allan.
January 29 at 10:15pm · Like

 **Kayla Lamb** He just walked in the days inn
January 29 at 10:15pm · Edited · Like · 👍7

 **Kayla Lamb** He found her! 😊
January 29 at 10:17pm · Like · 👍21

 **Ashley Sparks** Thank God
January 29 at 10:17pm · Like · 👍2

 **Calibabe Alltheway** Thank you Kayla - I will be praying for traveling mercies for Allan's safe return home in all these road conditions.
January 29 at 10:18pm · Like · 👍2

 **Calibabe Alltheway** Thank you Allan!! Just amazingly awesome!!!
January 29 at 10:18pm · Like · 👍3

 **Alice Broxton** Yayyyy!!!!! Now I feel like I can finally get some sleep 😊 thanks so much Kayla and Alan!
January 29 at 10:18pm · Like · 👍4

 **Anne Hajigeorgiou** God bless your dad. I have a 5 week old and 3 year old and this broke my heart.
January 29 at 10:19pm · Edited · Like · 👍6

 **Melissa Set Apart Lewis** Updates on Air and road travel

http://www.cbsatlanta.com/category/209305/traffic
January 29 at 10:19pm · Like · 👍1

**Jennifer McCann** Alan you are so generous! Amazing person! Thank you everyone!

January 29 at 10:20pm · Like · 👍37

 **Stacy Hodges Gonzales** Amazing how people pull together in a time of need!! God bless you all!!!

January 29 at 10:21pm · Like · 👍6

 **Tish Imstillstanding Hammonds** Alan plz make sure you let us know when you make it home safely. God bless you!

January 29 at 10:27pm · Like · 👍5

---

## School Buses

The story of the school buses during Snow Storm 1 deserves a whole book on its own. I really cannot do it justice here, but I will briefly detail my perspective on it.

From very early on in the group, so many moms were posting on the site - frantic - because they could not get any current information on the school buses. Their children had not arrived home, were hours late, and no one knew where the buses were. I could not imagine being one of those moms, not knowing where their children were.

I spent a lot of time trying to get updates on the school buses but was unable to get much solid information. There were lots of rumors flying around the group – there was a story that one school bus had arrived at a Mexican restaurant, and the children had been taken from the bus into the restaurant to be fed and to use the bathroom but that "rules" had dictated that they could not stay there due to the fact that the restaurant sold alcohol, so the children were back stranded on a bus in the cold.

There were horrific stories coming in all night long of school buses stranded and in dire need of help. Rumors came in about a special needs bus stranded by a Mexican Restaurant in Smyrna. This was later confirmed by a Marietta Daily Journal article by Hannah Morgan January 30, 2014 09:01 PM:

State Rep. David Wilkerson (D-Austell), who has children at Smyrna's Russell Elementary and Mableton's Floyd Middle, spent the night with stranded school bus in a parking lot off of South Cobb Drive.

After leaving the Capitol at about 1 p.m. Tuesday, Wilkerson made his way out of the city along the back roads and didn't come to a complete halt until he reached the Cobb County line.

Wilkerson made it through traffic and reached a Publix at the corner of South Cobb Drive and the East-West Connector, where he saw a Cobb school bus. He walked over to the bus, and was blown away by what he saw.

Inside, there were five special-needs students, waiting with their bus driver.

"I was more than impressed. It's tough. You are dealing with potential medical issues, a lack of food and trying to get these kids home," he said.

He noticed dozens of people had taken shelter and were asleep in a nearby Mexican restaurant. By midnight, the bus had left, but another one sought safety in the parking lot.

This second bus had two special-needs students on it, a bus driver and a staff member.

A police officer came by and offered to shuttle the students to a hospital or the Smyrna Community Center. The bus driver was in contact with the children's parents, Wilkerson said, and everyone remained calm.

Wilkerson returned to the Mexican restaurant at sunrise, and when he came back to the parking lot, the bus was gone. The mother of one of the students called him at 7:30 a.m., just as her child got home.

In fact, there were a number of reports of buses containing children with special needs stranded throughout the night..

 **Kimberly Thompson Hulbert** There was a special needs bus with 2 kids stranded near me just a bit ago off Sewell Mill.
January 28 at 11:27pm · Like

More stories about school buses stranded flooded the site:

 **Yvonne McGary Cummings** My cousin just got her son home. Her brother walked two and a half miles to get him. A lady offered food to then but the driver was unable to let them eat it.
January 28 at 11:52pm · Like · 👍 1

 **Lisa Overstreet** It is true. One seen on Powers Ferry so I called all the Tv stations. One confirmed they knew of six. Said they were waiting for calls back from school districts. Called Ga Patrol and they promised to send an officer. Can't believe this is not the TOP concern of our leaders!
January 28 at 11:53pm · Like · 👍 18

 **Sabrina Lewis Johnson** Last I heard they are still out there the roads are just impassable
January 28 at 11:54pm · Like · 👍 1

 **Jerry Karpinski** Sad to say but yes it is true, fox 5 has reported it as well ☹
January 28 at 11:54pm · Like

 **Heather Merritt Chapman** the bus driver wouldnt let them eat it!? That is OUTRAGEOUS. This is an emergency situation and that if that was my child I would lose it on someone
January 28 at 11:56pm · Like · 👍 9

 **Leon Schmitz** My wife is on nb 400 not moving due to the accident at 9 and there is a bus full of kids next to her.
January 28 at 11:56pm · Like · 👍 3

 **Jacob Michael Coley** I saw a Fulton county bus pass by Dalrymple and Roswell road full
January 28 at 11:58pm · Like · 👍 2

 **Coleecia Cainion** My kids are still stranded at New Manchester High School (Douglas County) I'm trying to keep sane!!
January 28 at 11:58pm · Like

 **Melissa Cook** Oh my goodness this is making me cry
January 28 at 11:58pm · Like · 👍 4

 **Karen Nuckolls McClure** Mine were stranded at Milton High in North Fulton but a friend of my daughter took them in for the night!
January 28 at 11:59pm · Like

 **Amy Morrill Younkins** my husband was rescuing kids off buses about a half hour ago in roswell! so yes.
January 28 at 11:59pm · Like · 👍 5

 **Karen Nuckolls McClure** Poor babies!
January 28 at 11:59pm · Like

**David Knighton**

School bus 560 is behind me on 285s above camp creek and full of kids. Had a bag of oranges in my car I took back to them, not a 4 course meal but at least its something. Bus driver was very nice and seemed to be in pretty good spirits.

Like · Comment · January 29 at 1:51am

👍 Amy Williams, Kat-y Royale, Summer Finley and 1,858 others like this.

🔗 143 shares

💬 View previous comments                                        50 of 301

 **Danielle Streeter** The original post that started this thread the kids have been rescued but I saw a new post 20 mins ago of another bus (#617) on 285 around exit 25 near Sandy Springs with kids still stranded. They said a helicopter was hovering above the bus but that help on the ground still couldnt reach them
January 29 at 9:19am · Edited · Like · 👍 4

 **Karla Velasquez Luongo** Omg. Thank u danielle
January 29 at 8:53am · Like

 **Danielle Streeter** Just told the bus has moved about 1 mile in the last 2 hours and that ANOTHER bus is stranded at exit 24 as well
January 29 at 8:54am · Like

 **Danielle Streeter** Was told the bus around exit 25 is #617, havent heard of the bus # around exit 24
January 29 at 8:55am · Unlike · 👍 1

 **Kaity Rose White** There's a bus by a checkers stranded off camp creek posted the number to hwy patrol this is sad
January 29 at 9:06am · Unlike · 👍 1

 **Kaity Rose White** I keep trying to bump the post but idk
January 29 at 9:07am · Like

 **Danielle Streeter** whats the bus#? so it doesnt get confused with rescued buses. Are there kids in it?
January 29 at 9:08am · Like

 **Karla Ivon** At least is daylight now, thank God. That is, a plus.
January 29 at 9:09am · Like · 👍 5

 **Alexandra Wright** This is so awful. I feel for those poor kids and their terrified parents!! How unacceptable. This is Atlanta, for God's sake, this weather happens rarely!! It's just not worth all of this. All schools should have been closed! This has taught me a lesso... See More
January 29 at 9:19am · Like · 👍 6

 **David Knighton** Yes ● Kayla Reece Mejia I am
January 29 at 9:20am · Like · 👍 2

 **Kayla Reece Mejia** My husband is too. You probably won't be able to see him but just in case, he is driving a white 2500 HD chevy silverado. Large tires black wheels.
January 29 at 9:22am · Like

 **Kayla Reece Mejia** I know he is running low on fuel.
January 29 at 9:23am · Like

**Faith Imstill Standing Brown**

my kids are still stuck on a school bus I can imagine they are cold n tired it's bus 48 that left out of a philp Randolph elementary n south fulton county pray for me n my kids

Like · Comment · January 29 at 1:16am near Ben Hill, GA

👍 Cherie Welch, Mahaganey God'schild, DeOnar Gilbert and 386 others like this.

📄 53 shares

 **Shirley Wolfe** Yes authorities say they r top priority
January 29 at 3:04am · Like · 👍2

 **Beverly Langford** thank you
January 29 at 3:04am · Like

 **Angie Livingston Betsill** The Guard is on there way...the GA State Patrol is having to move stranded cars to even get the help to them. They know where the bus is and they are coming.
January 29 at 3:04am · Like · 👍11

 **Faith Imstill Standing Brown** to the person saying walk if I could I woulda been did that the road can't be walked to I've tried n yes same old same old
January 29 at 3:05am · Like · 👍4

 **Camille Dent** LORD JESUS I HOPE THE HEAT IS STILL RUNNING AND I HOPE THOSE BABIES ARE NOW SLEEPING. I KNOW THEY ARE EXHAUSTED.
January 29 at 3:05am · Like · 👍4

 **Tamyetta Fuller** New Hope is between Cascade and Campbellton.
January 29 at 3:05am · Like · 👍1

 **Faith Imstill Standing Brown** yeah but his work stops before my house in this place we are fulton county not city of Atlanta so the national guard n fulton county police is handling it
January 29 at 3:06am · Like

 **Faith Imstill Standing Brown** first problem for the first 7 hours no one could tell me the exact location of the bus they just knew it ran into some trouble after it left with the kids but couldn't make contact smh
January 29 at 3:08am · Like · 👍2

 **Danielle Streeter** If this is #560, I heard they are located on 285s near New Hope Rd
January 29 at 3:08am · Like · 👍1

 **Tamyetta Fuller** Good National Guard on the way. I'm waiting for my husband he's been on the road home from Cartersville since 1pm.
January 29 at 3:09am · Like

 **Danielle Streeter** A good samaritan in a car in front of the bus has given them a bag of oranges to eat and is continuing to check on them
January 29 at 3:09am · Like · 👍6

 **Faith Imstill Standing Brown** if I woulda knew before dark exactly where they where I coulda got to them maybe but after dark they shut down all these streets n yes the bus number is 560 apparently the route number is 48 what station are y'all listening to please cause I'm not getting

**Tonya Winters**

Hi buys I am beside myself my son is on Fulton County Schools bus #4226 stuck between Cascade and Campbellton,no food no water on the bus 13 hours. Anybody have any info?

Unlike · Comment · January 29 at 4:29am

👍 You and 8 others like this.

🔲 3 shares

 **Alexis June** Is this a Westlake high school bus? I can check my email updates
January 29 at 4:32am · Like

 **Chyron Volinski** Gosh how could they let this happen. In my prayers
January 29 at 4:33am · Like · 👍 1

 **Tonya Winters** Yes Alexis Riverwood H S bus headed to Westlake
January 29 at 4:33am · Like

 **Lis Barrett** Tonya Winters check SnowedOutSouthAtlanta as well
January 29 at 4:34am · Like

 **Laura Tate** Bump
January 29 at 4:35am · Like · 👍 1

 **Tonya Winters** Bump
January 29 at 4:38am · Like

 **Tonya Winters** Lisa Barrett can you send me the invite to that group
January 29 at 4:39am · Like

 **Michelle Sollicito** Oh gosh - I cannot imagine how I would feel if my kids were on a bus and not home right now
January 29 at 4:39am · Like · 👍 1

 **Brian Follens G** Check the news websites or call the National Guard. Busses are a priority
January 29 at 4:39am · Like · 👍 3

 **Michelle Sollicito** https://www.facebook.com/groups/413082885492699/

 **SnowedOutSouthAtlanta**
1,009 members

January 29 at 4:39am · Like · 👍 1 · Remove Preview

 **Michelle Sollicito** just go to the url and I will approve u
January 29 at 4:40am · Like · 👍 2

 **Marla Ingram** Praying for them!! And for peace for you!!
January 29 at 4:41am · Like

 **Alexis June** Tje update says that bus us still stranded and the national guard is in route to help on 285
January 29 at 4:41am · Unlike · 👍 6

 **Alexis June** I received that update at 0347
January 29 at 4:42am · Unlike · 👍 1

Updates were posted about school buses overnight but Tonya's son was still not anywhere safe.

**Danielle Streeter**

PARENTS WITH KIDS ON BUSES: There is a bus (#560) full of kids off 285s near Camp Creek and New Hope Rd. A good samaritan has given them a bag of oranges from his car and continuing to check on them but if anyone else can assist with blankets, food, water, warm clothing...please!! Im sure these parents are worried sick and I cant imagine how scared these kids are.

Are there anymore buses of children still out there that need help?

Update: Mother of child on #4226 posted that she received a call letting her know that police were rescuing the kids off the bus

Update: Nat'l Guard and police helped #502 get to a Kroger on Cascade for food and shelter

Update: Fulton County bus #4226 could still be stranded on 285 near Cascade & Campbellton

Update: #560 has arrived back at school, but #502 is still on the road...

Unlike · Comment · January 29 at 2:28am · Edited

👍 You, DeOnar Gilbert, Ronika Brooks and 118 others like this.

🔁 99 shares

💬 View previous comments                                    50 of 122

 **Maryann Day** Listening to the news right now and a mother is on saying her kids are still on the buses.. Her two children are 15 and 17 and cell phones have died so she can no longer contact them Has not spoken to them in 2 hours... Praying for these kids.. They said they are hungry and had to use the bathroom.
January 29 at 4:11am · Like · 👍 2

 **Sharmon McCard Johnson** praying for them all
January 29 at 4:12am · Like · 👍 1

 **Lauren Stanford Novak** 😊 my husband just called me (he's national guard) .... They will get those babies! They are on their way!
January 29 at 4:12am · Like · 👍 18

 **Macy Diehl** Cassandra, my heart and prayers go out to you. I can't imagine what a long night it has been for you!
January 29 at 4:13am · Like · 👍 3

 **Cassandra Jackson** Lauren, please tell your husband that I said, "THANK YOU from the bottom of my heart!"
January 29 at 4:14am · Edited · Like · 👍 6

 **Amy Duran Palmer** OMG I can't imagine! Cassandra prayers to you

Kids with special needs were stranded on buses without food or water, and "rules" prevented the school bus drivers from allowing the kids to get help.

**Sabrina Nassar**

This bus was stranded outside our house from 4:00 yester day and currently is still here. In the bus was a bus driver who was not going to take the risk to drive up this icy hill with SPECIAL NEEDS kids inside. Thankfully, some of the parents walked for miles and came to get their kids. It was 10:30 at night and the last Childs mom was stuck in traffic with a 3 year old in the back seat, she was trying to pick up her 4 year old son. So my mom constantly tried getting the bus driver and young child to come out of the bus and into our house so they could use the bathroom. On the last try to convince them, she made the bus driver call the school and the Childs parents and asked if they could come in our house. Finally the school said yes and the mother was totally fine with it. Now here is the crazy part. A couple hours later the police arrived at our house. Because "he was told" by the parents that there was a stranded bus with kids on it but he thought they were "joking" and he was not taking it seriously. Not to mention the bus is only being held by FOUR firewood logs to stop it from rolling down the hill. My sibling and a couple other teenagers pfrom the neighborhood were outside for 6 hours offering places to stay and telling them which roads to stay off of and that the best idea was to leave their cars and walk home if they love close. We constantly had to push cars out of the way without slipping on the I've ourselves. I'm thankful that there is some people out there that actually want to take action in helping others.

Eventually, Tonya got information about her son's school bus, thanks to State Senator Vincent Fort appealing via our site, but it was traumatic waiting with her to find out where it was and how her son was doing..

Jennifer McKenna "Danielle Streeter: Senator Vincent Fort is looking for more accurate info on the location of #4226. If anyone has any additional info on this bus please post!!"
January 29 at 5:35am · Like · 👍 1

Alexis June I have his number, I can call him.
January 29 at 6:46am · Like

Alexis June Last update was 0633, 5 Buses made it back to Wrstlake 4226 is NOT one
January 29 at 6:48am · Like

Alexis June The buses are 547, 813,814,826 and 4156
January 29 at 6:50am · Like

Alexis June They hope tp try and get thiae students back out on busea by 10 am, to get them home
January 29 at 6:51am · Like

Kelly O'Connor Morgan Praying you find the bus.
January 29 at 6:54am · Like

Tamara Greenwood Some bus is at the Kroger on Cascade Road.
January 29 at 7:06am · Like · 👍 2

Tamara Greenwood Many buses were rescued and taken to the Cascade Kroger. CBS News Atlanta is reporting on it now.
January 29 at 7:07am · Like · 👍 3

Natalie Hicks Lagace B
January 29 at 7:56am · Like

Laura Tate Bump
January 29 at 8:05am · Like

Tonya Winters 4226 is at Cascade Kroger any ideas who is in charge and how we get them home I talk to my son and he is fine just tired and hungry how about anyone else
January 29 at 9:43am · Like · 👍 2

Write a comment...

Shortly after the post above, Tonya got her son home. But we got further confirmation that more school buses were still stranded that morning (Wednesday):

 **Becky Atkinson**

KATHY ATKINSON POST!!!!!!!285 IN ATLANTA BESIDE EXIT 25 SANDY SPRINGS , NEED HELP IN THIS AREA . LIKE A BIG PARKING LOT ON HIGHWAY , SCHOOL BUS FULL OF CHILDREN , NEWS HELICOPTER HOVERING FOR 15 OR MORE MINUTES BUT NO EMERGENCY VEHICLES CAN GET TO PEOPLE TO HELP !!!!!

Like · Comment · January 29 at 8:16am · Edited

👍 11 people like this.

📝 16 shares

**Danielle Streeter** Whats the bus # or school these kids are from?
January 29 at 8:18am · Like · 👍 1

**Tanya Rials Gault** I am at Exit 24. My house backs up to 285. Anything we can do to help!!!
January 29 at 8:22am · Like · 👍 2

**Kathy Atkinson** im told a helicopter is there now hovering for about 15 mins , i cant get my friends on their cell anymore to ask bus number
January 29 at 8:24am · Like · 👍 1

**Danielle Streeter** someone else posted that bus was rescued around 3am...can you confirm that this bus is a current situation and not an old one so that the word can be spread if these kids still need help?
January 29 at 8:37am · Edited · Like

**Becky Atkinson** ok ill check..
January 29 at 8:38am · Like · 👍 1

**Becky Atkinson** SHE IS CHECKING TO MAKE SURE, AND WILL BE ANSWERING UR POST!!
January 29 at 8:44am · Like

**Danielle Streeter** Thanks
January 29 at 8:46am · Like

**Jay Tkm Yahaira** I like 3 minutes off the exit ): omg
January 29 at 8:47am · Like

**Kathy Atkinson** BUS 617 , TRAFFIC HAS BEEN MOVING SO BUS HAS NOT BEEN SEEN SINCE 7 AM BEFORE EXIT 22 ON 285, ALSO ANOTHER BUS ON EXIT 24 STRANDED BUT NOT SURE OF NUMBER
January 29 at 8:49am · Like

**Kathy Atkinson** got my friends on the phone , they were moving about a mile but now at a stand still again but a mile in a long time tho
January 29 at 8:51am · Like

Unsurprisingly perhaps, but unbeknownst to me, many local and state government figures had now joined the site.  Representatives Roger Bruce and Sharon Cooper, both of whom I had had contact with on previous occasions (Sharon Cooper is my representative), were both on the site by Wednesday morning for example.  Kathleen Angelucci, a CCSD (Cobb County School District) School Board member who I knew fairly well from my educational advocacy work, had also been on the SnowedOutAtlanta site most of the night, frantically working on getting the school buses home using some of the information and updates from the SnowedOutAtlanta group, making calls to the National Guard and calling CCSD Operations Chief and Deputy Superintendent Chris Ragsdale (who ended up staying at work 36 hours to get kids home from school), in an attempt to get the school kids home as quickly as possible.

Kathleen Angelucci and Chris Ragsdale deserve special recognition for the intense efforts they put in that night getting most kids home by 2 a.m. They did all this work under the radar, not asking for recognition of any kind, not doing it for any political purpose, but I want to commend them for how hard they worked.

Despite all their incredible efforts, and the efforts of other school districts across Atlanta, it was not until lunchtime next day that all 99 stranded Atlanta school buses were reported to have reached safety of some kind. It was a traumatic night for all parents involved.

 **Lisa Overstreet**
Fox News has reported that the 99 school buses loaded with children stranded on the roads last night at midnight have been rescued and are safe! I also received independent confirmation that the stranded bus on Powers Ferry is no longer there! Praying this is correct and the children are now warm and safe!!!

Like · Comment · January 29 at 12:45pm near North High Shoals, GA

It soon came to light how heroic some of the school bus drivers had been in their efforts to keep the children safe. It is stressful enough driving a school bus full of children without all the added stresses of them all being cold, hungry, thirsty, desperate for the bathroom, very tired and pretty scared. Add to that the fact that the buses were often in great danger due to slippery roads and hills – as evidenced by the now famous "SnowedOut Video" which shows a school bus full of children seemingly about to be hit by a Marta bus sliding down a hill, see the video here: http://tinyurl.com/snowedoutvid

There is no doubt at all that the school bus drivers deserve medals for what they did that night. Despite numerous attempts to get names from the Cobb County School District I have been unable to obtain them. All I can do is say "thank you" on behalf of all parents of children in Cobb County. Cobb County School Board did award them, and other teachers and staff who worked throughout that night, extra pay for their troubles, but it just does not seem enough:

MARIETTA — Roughly 1,500 Cobb School District employees will be getting larger pay checks in the coming months with the school board's Thursday decision recognizing the bus drivers, teachers and staff who worked through the Jan. 28 snowstorm.

Superintendent Michael Hinojosa asked the board to approve rewarding the "noble and unselfish" contributions made by district staff during the January storm, many of whom spent the night on buses and in schools keeping watch over students.

*Superintendent Dr. Michael Hinojosa listens as several concerned parents speak about how they feel he handled the snow storm last Tuesday. Hinojosa announced his resignation from the Cobb school system later in the meeting.*

The board approved spending about $395,000 out of the district's general fund to pay more than 1,400 hourly employees, including bus drivers and maintenance staff, $25 for every hour worked after 3 p.m. Jan. 28 and into the next day.

Roughly 300 teachers and administrators who worked longer hours Jan. 28 will be paid one personal day by the end of the school year.

*(Hannah Morgan, February 28, 2014 04:00 AM, Marietta Daily Journal)*

We also must not forget the teachers who did an amazing job that night – many sleeping over with children in the gyms or cafeterias at the schools, making food for them, putting on videos for them to watch and trying to make them as comfortable as possible.

I know that my own children's principal (Ms. Karen Wacker) stayed late at their school (Eastvalley Elementary) with a couple of teachers, and then once all their children had made it home, she went on to Sedalia Park Elementary school with some students from Wheeler High School who had been stranded, and stayed overnight there looking after a number of students.

This was just one of the stories I heard from that night of teachers and principals going beyond the call of duty for students and their parents. It was not confined to public schools but was also prevalent at private schools that night.

One other story involving a principal going the extra mile that hit very close to home for me was that involving Jorge Carillo's family. Jorge was one of the many "strangers" I invited to stay at my home that night, if they could get through the snow to my house, but he was the only one who made it. This is the conversation I had with his wife over Facebook before he arrived:

**Claire Willeford-Carrillo**

January 28th, 7:44pm

Hey Michelle, thank you for accepting my request! I wanted to see if it is Ok for me to send my husband to you tonight... So kind and generous of you to offer, he has been on the road since 12:30 and hasn't moved from the area. It'd probably take him another couple of hours to get to you even though he's very nearby.

yes where is he

He said he is at fern street-- I sent him the address and he is almost right there!

It was much closer than I thought

Thank you so much, you don't know how much I appreciate your hospitality.

perfect

what is his name?

Jorge Carrillo. Thanks Michelle
☺☺☺☺

u r welcome

I hope he finds us

we are hard to find

wanna give him my number?

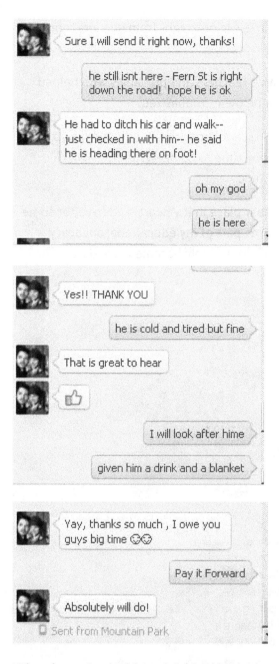

When he arrived, although he had had a long journey without food, water or a restroom, he was unconcerned about himself but desperately worried about his family. His daughters, previously homeschooled, had gone to Woodacres school (a private school) that day for the first time ever, so they didn't know anyone there very well. But his wife couldn't pick them up from school because she had crashed her car on her way to get them – with her baby son in the car. The crash his wife and son had experienced was worrying enough for Jorge, but now he had the added worry that he had been unable to pick up his daughters from the school, and he had no idea where they were.

A few calls were, however, enough to put his mind at rest. His wife and son were well despite the accident, and his daughters had been taken home by the principal of Woodacres school and were now having great fun at a "sleepover" at her house. I could see the emotion in Jorge's face when he was told the news by his wife, and I started crying myself. So much kindness in one night from one stranger to another was almost too much to take.

The level of gratitude I, and so many others felt and feel towards teachers and principals who helped that night – in fact, to *all* those who helped that night - cannot be over-emphasized.

I hope Cobb County residents remember the dedication of their school bus drivers, administrators and its teachers (working in both public and private sectors) for a long time to come. Without such wonderful, dedicated staff that night could have been catastrophic.

All the staff within the Cobb County education system hold a dear place in my heart, and have for some time, and I have spent a lot of time and effort fighting for them as part of my educational advocacy, mainly via my group "Fund Cobb Schools" on Facebook. That night, I simply became more determined and more resolved to continue that fight.

**Michelle Sollicito**

I just want to give a shout out to some people who really deserve recognition from the storm.

By far the people who deserve the most recognition, I feel, are the bus drivers who kept all those kids safe in extreme conditions. I cannot tell you how stressful it is to be a bus driver with 20-40 kids who have not eaten, drunk, been to the bathroom in 12 hours and are FROZEN too. Bus drivers did everything they could to keep those kids safe and they are the true heroes of this whole situation.

Also, the teachers who went way beyond their job descriptions to ensure the safety of the children. I am trying to get more names, but I know staff at EastValley, Sedalia Park, Wheeler and other schools stayed overnight to watch kids whose parents could not get to them. In particular, Ms Wacker (Karen) who not only stayed late at EastValley ensuring the safety of the kids at her school, but once she was done with that, she walked through the snow about half a mile down to Sedalia Park and stayed all night there with children from Sedalia Park.

These are the true heroes of the storm and I want us to remember this if and when we are asked to pay the extra school millage rate that I think is inevitable to take the millage rate up to 20%. Remember these teachers have taken huge effective pay cuts over recent years, yet they pay us back with such selfless service.

The corporation that deserves most recognition I feel was Home Depot - once we on this site found out that Home Depot was offering shelter, food and drink to anyone who could make it to their stores, we spread that news like wildfire, and I received thousands of messages saying how great Home Depot were.

Like · Comment · February 3 at 11:45am

# The Numbers

Amount of actual snowfall: 2.6 inches (20th heaviest recorded in Atlanta)

Number of traffic accidents: 1000+ (no one really knows, many were not reported)

Number of deaths in GA related to weather: 2

Flights cancelled: 2600

Number of warnings given by National Weather Service in the days leading up to the storm: 6-8

## North and Central Georgia Winter Storm
### January 28-29, 2014

### NWS Product Timeline

312 PM Sun, Jan 26, 2014
* Winter Storm Watch Issued for central Georgia - including south Atlanta metro from 10 AM Tuesday until 1 PM (product text; map)

315 PM Sun, Jan 26, 2014
* Briefing emailed to government and media partners (pdf)

453 AM Mon, Jan 27, 2014
* Winter Storm Watch expanded to include the entire metro Atlanta area (product text; map)

835 AM Mon, Jan 27, 2014
* Tweet issued "Conf increasing for significant snow moving in rush hour Tues. Dont wait to make plans for work/school"

100 PM Mon, Jan 27, 2014
* Webinar given to government and media partners(pdf)

308 PM Mon, Jan 27, 2014
* Tweet issued "Winter precip will make travel risky across GA midday Tues into Weds. Not a bad idea to stay off the roads if you're able!"

322 PM Mon, Jan 27, 2014
* Winter Storm Warning issued for central Georgia - including south Atlanta metro area (product text; map)
* Winter Storm Watch remains in effect for rest of metro Atlanta (product text; map)

## The Maps

The Google maps were an extremely important part of SnowedOutAtlanta on Snow Storm 1 – possibly the single most useful part of the whole group – and yet they did not get much attention in the national news headlines that followed about SnowedOutAtlanta.

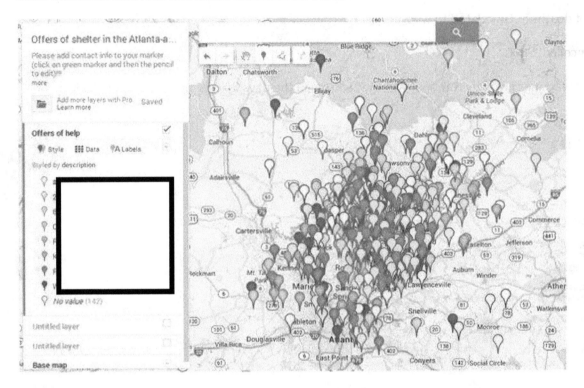

Not only did they enable people very quickly to find shelter near to where they were located, they held up under the extreme load very well (50,000 people were accessing the map to either add shelters or find shelters that night) and they were relatively easy for people to use. I honestly think that what Jelena Crawford did in creating the Google Maps that night for the people of Atlanta is at least as important as what I did, and I wish she was being honored for her maps the way I am being honored for SnowedOutAtlanta.

I know that part of the success of SnowedOutAtlanta in averting a catastrophe that night – a night that I think could easily have otherwise been Atlanta's Katrina, or Atlanta's 9/11 - was because of the amount of emotional support people out in the cold received just from knowing that there were 50,000 people out there who cared whether or not they lived or died.

Seeing a map on which literally hundreds of people were offering their homes as shelter, and so many businesses were offering their premises as shelter, was surely a large part of that, especially given that so few "official" shelters were open.

There was a beautiful spirit within the SnowedOutAtlanta group during Snow Storm 1 night. The general feeling was one of love, openness, trust and caring for others. The spirit was a little infectious and some became almost addicted to helping people that night while others seemed carried away on a kind of euphoria.

Throughout Snow Storm 1, I received messages offering me gifts or money to thank me for SnowedOutAtlanta. I was offered massages, manicures, vacations – even a house and a car! Very early on I made a public message indicating that I would not accept any payment of any kind for the site.

**Michelle Sollicito**

I recognize that there are a lot of people who feel they want to do something to pay me back for this site. I am extremely grateful for that and will try to work with someone like the Red Cross to arrange some way to allow you guys to thank me by paying it forward to them - something along those lines. Again, please note that anyone selling tshirts or asking for any money whatsoever does not have my permission and it has nothing to do with me.

Later, I developed a relationship with the Red Cross and asked people to specifically pay it forward by giving blood.

Please, if you were helped by this site, consider Paying It Forward by giving blood.

From the Red Cross - we really need blood and platelet donations. This week's weather alone cancelled more than 1,800 Red Cross blood and platelet donations in our area - this coupled with more than 20,000 donations cancelled this month because of weather nationwide means we need donors now more than ever. Most of our sites are open this afternoon, and we hope to be back to (mostly) normal operations tomorrow. You can visit www.redcrossblood.org and enter your zip for locations near you. Or, call 1-800-RED CROSS."

**I felt it was extremely important to the ethos of the group that no one would think I had any ulterior motive behind creating or running the group. I did not want to spoil the group by making money from it in any way – or even by *appearing to* make money from it in any way. At intervals throughout the night I posted messages like this one:**

**Michelle Sollicito**
38 minutes ago

Just wanna make something clear. While its lovely to receive offers of gifts and money (thank you everyone) I really do not want anything in return for this PLEASE. It is important noone thinks there is some selfish motive involved in this as it might cloud the whole thing. So if ANYONE is asking anyone for money on my behalf, it is totally unauthorized by me and I DO NOT WANT IT TO HAPPEN! Simply Pay It Forward please

71 Likes  3 Comments

It was incredible to see how the "Pay It Forward" spirit pervaded the group all night long and people pledged to spread the spirit throughout Atlanta. Ever since, I have heard of so many stories of people being on the receiving end of pledges made that night on the site, and also on the Pay It Forward group that sprang out of SnowedOutAtlanta.

Massage therapists have given free massages to the poor and needy, countless members gave blood in the days shortly after the crisis, food and money was given to homeless people and those who were down on their luck, and many many gofundme accounts sprang from the group to help others.

# Chapter 2 – Snow Storm 2

In between Snow Storm 1 (January 28-29th) and Snow Storm 2 (February 11-12th), I closed the SnowedOutAtlanta group to new posts and made it a "secret group" which meant that existing members were the only ones who could see the content, and members could no longer post to the group. I made the decision to close the group because I noticed that the wonderful spirit the group had encapsulated so well over the "emergency" period had ebbed and was being replaced by negativity. Looking back, I believe that the decision to close it for that period of time was a good one.

However, I made it clear when I closed it that if another emergency were to happen, I would re-open the group. Knowing that Atlanta had not seen an emergency like this one in years, I anticipated the group would not open until at least the start of tornado season. How wrong I was!

Just as we were all recovering from Snow Storm 1, weather reports started to suggest an even more severe storm – this time an *ice* storm, not a snow storm - was about to hit us. At first, it seemed the predictions might not be accurate, but I am in a lot of groups in the utilities industry and I started to note panic coming from those who were based in Atlanta, and other areas that would be affected by this storm, so I realized this could be serious.

After Snow Storm 1, I had attended a CERT course (Community Emergency Response Training), done some FEMA certifications and had made a lot of contacts in the Emergency Management community in an attempt to prepare myself to support people if such an emergency happened again.

However, I had not anticipating needing to be prepared so soon after the first storm.

With the knowledge that a new severe storm was about to hit the Atlanta area, I frantically gathered all the resources and contacts I could find to help prepare people for this second storm.

I had asked some of the group members to accumulate suggestions and posts about how to compile an Emergency Kit together (see Appendix for some of the best posts on this topic) so that we could choose the best recommendations and consolidate these into one document. There was no time for fine-tuning now, so I cobbled together a post with recommendations and put it in the "Pinned Post" (see the Appendix for examples of the Pinned Post's contents).

I had asked another member to write an article about Weather radios and CB/Ham radio choices also. Again, there was no time for polish so we simply put together what we could and posted it.

I posted a number of links to useful "Disaster Preparedness" content that Apogee Interactive had provided for its utility clients and while I was doing so I found other useful content on Utility websites.

Similarly, I found content on GEMA and FEMA websites and linked to that within the "Pinned Post" also.

# The Calm Before The Storm

The second storm was a very different experience to the first storm.  For one thing, people had very recently been very badly burned by not being prepared and by not being cautious enough during the first storm: they were not going to make that mistake again in a hurry!

Atlanta public schools, Cobb County schools and Fulton County schools were all closed all day Tuesday February 11th even though no ice or snow hit those areas until late on Tuesday evening.

Residents were warned not to "fall into a lull of relaxation" because only rain fell during the day on Tuesday. Clear, all-agency messages and press releases (from GEMA, Governor Deal, the police departments, the weather forecasters, etc.) used alarming language to describe the upcoming storm. The Weather Center predicted a "Catastrophic Ice Storm" and the Georgia Power Emergency spokesperson warned of 250,000 – 300,000 outages, saying "In 30 years of living in Georgia, I've never seen an inch of ice fall."

**Scott Janz**

Press Conference: Georgia Power Emergency Spokesman just announced that major outages will occur. 250,000 - 300,000 could be without power. "In 30 years of living in Georgia, I've never seen an inch of ice fall". Governor "People in Atlanta that saw rain today, shouldn't fall into a lull of relaxation".

Like · Comment · February 11 at 3:23pm near Atlanta, GA

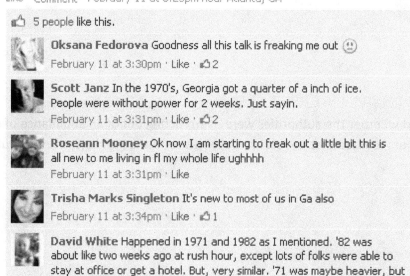

5 people like this.

**Oksana Fedorova** Goodness all this talk is freaking me out 🙁
February 11 at 3:30pm · Like · 👍 2

**Scott Janz** In the 1970's, Georgia got a quarter of a inch of ice. People were without power for 2 weeks. Just sayin.
February 11 at 3:31pm · Like · 👍 2

**Roseann Mooney** Ok now I am starting to freak out a little bit this is all new to me living in Fl my whole life ughhhh
February 11 at 3:31pm · Like

**Trisha Marks Singleton** It's new to most of us in Ga also
February 11 at 3:34pm · Like · 👍 1

**David White** Happened in 1971 and 1982 as I mentioned. '82 was about like two weeks ago at rush hour, except lots of folks were able to stay at office or get a hotel. But, very similar. '71 was maybe heavier, but fewer cars around then, so traffic not so much. Both cases, no power for about a week.

Utilities warned of the possibility of mass outages:

**Samantha Walker**

\*\*\*EMAIL FROM WALTONEMC\*\*\*

Several different forecasts and forecasters are in agreement that Walton EMC's service area has a high probability of seeing 1/4 inch or more of ice accumulation on Wednesday with the National Weather Service commenting in their forecast discussion that we could see the most significant ice storm in 10 to 20 years. If this comes true, you can expect widespread power outages with the severity and duration dependent on the thickness of the ice.

You may have a small window to make last minute preparations on Tuesday. Rest assured that your cooperative is preparing and will do its best to restore power as quickly as possible in the event of a widespread outage. If ice totals approach 1/4 to 1/2 inch or more and roads become impassable, you should be prepared for a multi-day outage event.

While we do not seek to cause undue alarm, we do feel that our customer-owners should be fully informed as to the possible impact of a major ice storm and resulting power outages.

Outage Website- http://www.outageentry.com/dvOSM /dvOSM2.php?Client=WALTON

 **Outage Status Map**
outageentry.com
You must enable Javascript on your browser to check your power status or report a power outage. Click here for JavaScript help.

Like · Comment · Share · February 11 at 10:57am

Although some wondered whether the authorities were overreacting out of an abundance of caution due to recent events, others realized that this storm really was something to be worried about.

**Dena Sims**

I am curious what you all think, cast your opinion. Is this storm hype or really going to ba problem? By the way, I am prepared, just wondering

Like · Comment · February 11 at 1:25am

👍 5 people like this.

 **Michele Holbrook Haley** Super Bad, trees falling on power lines and lots of ice, Stay Safe.
February 11 at 1:27am · Like · 👍1

 **Jeanie Stein** It's gonna be worse because of the ice involved this time!
February 11 at 1:28am · Like · 👍2

 **Colleen Maureen** It's too soon to say. We're not even at the big start of this storm yet. But I would say it will be a big deal because there's a virtually unanimous verdict that this will be a major storm that has far worse repercussions than the last storm, i.e. more ice, downed trees and power lines and prolonged power outages.
February 11 at 1:29am · Edited · Like · 👍3

 **Melissa Rushton** In my opinion I think it's a little of both. I do think there will be some damage from it. Perhaps not as bad as last time as far as traffic goes because a lot more people are prepared. But, since this storm is so close to the last one, I think there i... See More
February 11 at 1:29am · Like · 👍6

 **Dena Sims** Michele, the reason I am asking is I think it has the potential to be bad with a few days without power. People at work are saying not.
February 11 at 1:29am · Like · 👍1

 **Michele Holbrook Haley** In 2005 I was stuck inside 6 days and no power for 5, it might get serious like that again. Dressed in 4 layers of clothes and stayed under blankets, they key is put something on your head will keep you warmer. 😃
February 11 at 1:30am · Like · 👍3

 **Dena Sims** I would rather be wrong and prepared than not and then in a hurt. Lol.
February 11 at 1:30am · Like · 👍7

Most people anticipated power outages and prepared for them nonetheless, given the weather forecasters' usage of terms such as "catastrophic ice storm" and their warnings that there could be "power outages for several days…"

**Trevor Picciano** shared Weather Center- North & West Georgia's status.

\* Share with Friends & Family \*

**Weather Center- North & West Georgia**

This Winter Storm is among one of the most challenging forecasts most meteorologists have ever faced. There are so many different elements that are coming into play, creating the "Perfect Storm" … Unfortunately, there will likely be a Catastrophic Ice Storm for Northern and Central Georgia, starting tomorrow morning…

If you haven't prepared, you are deeply encouraged to prepare immediately. We could be dealing with power outages for several days… Traveling is not advised after midnight tonight, so stay off the roads! Wherever you are late tonight, plan on being there for at least a day or two, until the roads begin to clear up. School systems will likely remained closed through the rest of the week for much of the area. A State of Emergency will remain in effect until Further Notice … There is a high threat of falling trees and power lines, due to heavy ice accumulations… The key is Preparation… "Expect the worst, while still hoping for the best"… Everyone is encouraged to charge their phones tonight and only use them in the event of an emergency. Power Outages could start early in the day tomorrow and we don't know how long we could be without power. Not everyone will lose power, but there is a high potential that there will be widespread outages. This Winter Storm is being labeled as a "Once in a Lifetime Event"… That alone, should stress the severity of the potential crisis situation we are expecting to face …

Well-informed members helped others by posting information that would prove useful to many later when they did, indeed, experience power outages.

**Susan Hostrup Montgomery**

Just signed up for Georgia Power alerts so if I lose power I will know estimated time of restoration. Sign up here: http://georgiapower.com /in-your-community/storm-center/home.cshtml

**Overview | In Your Community | Georgia Power**
georgiapower.com

When an outage occurs, you can count on Georgia Power to provide you with the highest level of service as we work hard to restore your power.

Like · Comment · Share · February 11 at 11:18am

Write a comment…

## Melissa Set Apart Lewis

**nage Your Communications from Georgia Power**

**ver Outage Communications**

eive updates on the status of your power outage including estimated times of restoration, cause of the ge, and notification when the power has been restored. View Terms and Conditions

| Send To | | Do NOT contact me between (ET) | Pause/Resume | |
|---------|---|---|---|---|
| il Nanny | abcdefg@abcdef... ○HTML ○Plain Text | ☑ 11 PM ⌄ and 7 AM ⌄ | Pause | Remov |
| e Home | (111) 222-3333 | ☑ 1 AM ⌄ and 7 AM ⌄ | Resume | Remov |

ld a way to contact me (5 max)

Restore previous or **Save Chang**

### Sign Up for Outage Alerts | Customer Service | Georgia Power

georgiapower.com

Georgia Power is the largest subsidiary of Southern Company, one of the nation's largest generators of electricity. The company is an investor-owned, tax-paying utility, serving 2.3 million customers in 155 of 159 counties in Georgia. Georgia...

---

**Kathy Shaw Amos** shared Brookhaven Post's photo.
You might want to set this up while you can.

Sign up for Georgia Power Outage Alerts.

There are three types of outage alerts: Email, text and phone call. You choose how you want to be notified about power outages and specify any time(s) when you would prefer NOT to be notified (such as times when you are asleep).

http://www.georgiapower.com/about/outage-alerts-video.cshtml

---

Many used the "calm before the storm" to ask questions in preparation for potential outages. There were questions about where to buy firewood, generators and non-electric space heaters. Many people asked questions about the safety of using certain heaters and generators indoors, or of using fireplaces that had not been used for some time.

**Elena Nicole**

I have a gas fireplace that is turned on with a light switch. It is completely enclosed with a glass front. My dad is concerned about opening the flue to release fumes but I don't see anywhere to do that! Any ideas?

**Jennifer Schmidt**

Sooooo....might be a silly question, but I'm a girl. Lol! I have a gas fireplace (there's a valve, not a switch) if the power goes out will I still be able to use the gas to light the fireplace? Be nice.

Like · Comment · February 11 at 4:43pm near Johns Creek, GA

Yasemin Yalcinkaya, Kat-y Royale and 31 others like this.

View previous comments                                             50 of 111

> **Gaye Pennington** I just asked that question 😊
> February 11 at 5:23pm · Like · 👍 1

> **Charles Todd Ingram** Yes you will.
> February 11 at 5:24pm · Like

> **Charles Todd Ingram** There are no silly questions
> February 11 at 5:24pm · Like

> **Cyndy Robedee** As long as the switch isn't electric. And who would be mean, thats a good question. 😊
> February 11 at 5:24pm · Like

> **Al Exler** Maybe there's an APP for that ?
> February 11 at 5:24pm · Like

> **Ashmurr Moran** A gas furnce need power but not sure bout fireplace
> February 11 at 5:26pm · Like

> **Jim Hannon** Look for a metal plate near the "logs" or under the burner that will give you the lighting instructions. Each unit is different and taking "general advice and recommendations" can only lead to no good when it comes to gas appliances.
> February 11 at 5:27pm · Like · 👍 1

> **Cordelia Ann Sheppard Riley** any vids on how this is done?
> February 11 at 5:27pm · Like

Personnel from the utility companies themselves also posted information to our group:

**Emily Matthews** via **Georgia Power**

Remember to utilize our online outage maps, outage alerts and other resources at www.georgiapower.com/storm. It's a mobile-friendly site and you can report an outage from your smartphone!

**Overview | In Your Community | Georgia Power**

georgiapower.com

Georgia Power is the largest subsidiary of Southern Company, one of the nation's largest generators of electricity. The company is an investor-owned, tax-paying utility, serving 2.3 million customers in 155 of 159 counties in Georgia. Georgia Power's rates remain well...

Like · Comment · Share · February 12 at 3:13pm

👍 3 people like this.

Write a comment...

Georgia Power had predicted more than 200,000 outages would occur and I believe the total was in fact pretty close to that. 113,000+ Georgia Power customers were affected by outages at the peak of the outages experienced and the AJC (Atlanta Journal Constitution) reported 150,000 total outages, but savvy members on the site kept totals that suggested the total was closer to 200,000, as they noticed that many news outlets were reporting only the maximum of Georgia Power customers (of course there are many utility companies serving Georgia although Georgia Power is by far the largest), or they were reporting the "peak" number and not the "total" number.

Members of the group were keeping close watch on the totals throughout the storm, right from the beginning:

**Kathy Burnett**

CNN is saying 54,000 people in Georgia without power already!

Like · Comment · February 12 at 9:05am

👍 5 people like this.

**Sarah Guest** Yeah...and that number only includes Georgia Power customers.

February 12 at 9:08am · Like · 👍1

**Arvind Hariharan** ☹

February 12 at 9:12am · Like

**Arvind Hariharan** Get prepared for worst. Just as a precautionary measure

February 12 at 9:12am · Like

**Ruth Brown Wilkes** Powerage outage is up to 80,000 now...be prepared.

February 12 at 10:16am · Like

During outages, members shared information to help those with no power get help in the most efficient manner possible. SMS tools were extremely useful to those who had lost power:

**Neda Abghari** text "GAPWR" the following commands to register, report etc ..... REG – To sign up to receive Outage Alerts.
OUT – To report an outage using your smartphone.
STAT – To check if there is a reported outage for a particular account. You can do this instead of waiting for an outage notification.
PAUSE – To stop receiving outage notifications temporarily.
RESUME – To re-start messaging for an account.
STOP – To terminate text communications from Georgia Power. This is a permanent stop (unlike PAUSE, which is temporary stop). Once this is done, you will need to re-register to start the communications again.
STOP ALL – To unsubscribe and stop receiving text messages from all accounts.
HELP – To obtain a list of text messaging keywords and the phone number to speak with a Customer Service Representative if you need assistance.
***Also not all service providers are included on the Smart Hub app... i just tried to use it for my GP account and it is not included.

February 12 at 11:43am · Edited · Like · 👍1

**Daniel Eaton** It was easy for me to sign up with SMS using the method above because my cell phone was already associated with my account. But if it is not, it is easier to sign up online. You can also add up to five different numbers so that other family members can report outages or get alerts when power is restored.

February 12 at 11:48am · Like · 👍1

But the outage numbers kept rising, and group members kept tracking those numbers as they rose.

**Marty Sharpe**
Georgia Power Outages, as of a few minutes ago..

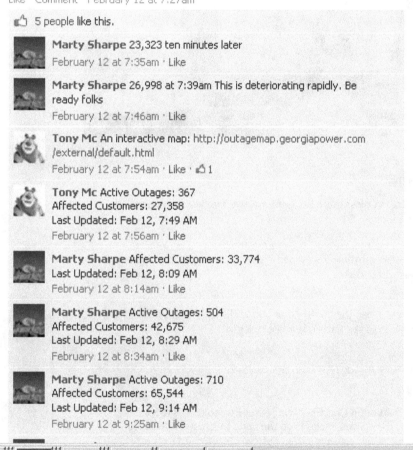

**Active Outages:** 233

**Affected Customers:** 20,085

**Last Updated:** Feb 12, 7:19 AM

*Information is updated every 10 minutes.*

Like · Comment · February 12 at 7:27am

👍 5 people like this.

**Marty Sharpe** 23,323 ten minutes later
February 12 at 7:35am · Like

**Marty Sharpe** 26,998 at 7:39am This is deteriorating rapidly. Be ready folks
February 12 at 7:46am · Like

**Tony Mc** An interactive map: http://outagemap.georgiapower.com/external/default.html
February 12 at 7:54am · Like · 👍1

**Tony Mc** Active Outages: 367
Affected Customers: 27,358
Last Updated: Feb 12, 7:49 AM
February 12 at 7:56am · Like

**Marty Sharpe** Affected Customers: 33,774
Last Updated: Feb 12, 8:09 AM
February 12 at 8:14am · Like

**Marty Sharpe** Active Outages: 504
Affected Customers: 42,675
Last Updated: Feb 12, 8:29 AM
February 12 at 8:34am · Like

**Marty Sharpe** Active Outages: 710
Affected Customers: 65,544
Last Updated: Feb 12, 9:14 AM
February 12 at 9:25am · Like

At first, even those who were experiencing outages seemed pretty calm, though used the group to ask questions:

**Candis Hughes Lazarre**

Does anyone know how to work this type fireplace? We're without power. I'm 8 months pregnant and have a pre schooler and 10year old. My husband and I have no idea how to use this. Our home is total electric. Is this just a wood fireplace or??? We're freezing! Our power went out a couple of hours ago.. any help would be appreciated. Thanks

Like · Comment · February 12 at 7:57am

 4 people like this.

 **Ashton Loyd** Unless there is a gas turn on/off valve near it, you just need some wood!
February 12 at 8:01am · Like · 👍 2

 **Courtney Steinmann** It's a wood fireplace. Looks just like mine and we are also total electric
February 12 at 8:01am · Like · 👍 3

 **Gail Hoover** Open the flue!!!! Your husband should take a flash light and shine it up to see if the flue is open/closed
February 12 at 8:03am · Like · 👍 6

 **Jason Fleury** And do NOT burn charcoal in it.
February 12 at 8:04am · Like · 👍 6

**Lynette Robinson** Check out this youtube video on gas fireplaces. I played it and the video zooms in on the parts that may be similar to yours. http://www.youtube.com/watch?v=324NHDv-yXU
February 12 at 8:04am · Like · 👍 3

 **Michelle Sollicito** Be careful - if it has not been used for a while, there might be all sorts in the chimney and the chimney could catch fire (and catch the house on fire). If you are sure the chimney is clean then make sure the flue is open otherwise the house will fill with smoke. You might want to try a small fire first to see what happens
February 12 at 8:04am · Like · 👍 10

Because most people were safe in their houses, it seemed at first that all the fear surrounding Snow Storm 2 had been unjustified.  But then, just as in Snow Storm 1, the pleas of desperation started to appear on the site.

Suddenly, there came a rush of desperate posts all at once on Tuesday night.

Some were more worrisome than others, like the one involving a young woman, who we will call Patsy (to protect her true identity) who had recently given birth to a child with complications who was being asked to leave Northside Hospital to make room for other moms even though her daughter was still in the hospital. Patsy was distraught at the idea of leaving her baby and going home (she lived a good distance from the hospital), knowing that due to the snow she might not be able to get back to the hospital to pump breast milk for her daughter the next day. She posted on the site asking for solutions.

I offered her a bed in my house for the night. In normal circumstances, my house is 15-20 minutes' drive from the hospital but of course, these circumstances were far from normal, and Patsy said she was (understandably) nervous that she would not be able to get to the hospital from my house next day. There were some who worried that Patsy not be for real (again, understandable given how some people misuse the internet), that her story might be a scam to get us to pay her hotel bills for her. I myself was not sure, so I confirmed as much of her story as I could do by calling the hospital, getting put through to Patsy's room and talking to Patsy herself.

For me, that confirmed that Patsy had at least recently given birth to a baby in the Maternity unit of Northside Hospital (the Women's Center). So I tried to find a way to pay her hotel bills.

While I was looking for a way, the magic of SnowedOutAtlanta re-surfaced. Ashleigh Graham, another member of SnowedOutAtlanta, offered to pay for Patsy's hotel bills. Not only for that night, but until the Saturday of that week – four nights in total! As if that was not enough, Ashleigh drove to pick up Patsy and her mother from the hospital and delivered them to their hotel room, ordering them Chinese food for dinner!

Again, I was reminded of the generosity of spirit within the group, and again I was blown away by it.

Later we got updates from Ashleigh and others telling us about Patsy's progress, and that of her baby. She was also later helped by the 4x4's Helping Atlanta group, who helped her get to and from the hospital until the snow disappeared.

**Ashleigh Graham**

For anyone looking for an update on ▮▮▮ who had given birth at Northside Hospital and needed a place to stay nearby so she would be able to pump for and see her baby until she was able to be released, ▮▮▮ has been safely relocated to a hotel nearby the hospital. For those who doubted ▮▮▮ s story, yes, she really did just give birth and really was in need of a hand. It was sad to see so many hurtful insinuations posted about a young lady who was reaching out for help, which was sorely needed. I picked her up from the hospital and she was just the sweetest and most gracious young lady. God is good!!

Like · Comment · February 12 at 12:03am near Atlanta, GA

👍 Laura George, Bina Cline, Stacie Christopher and 1,276 others like this.

💬 View previous comments                                    50 of 190

**Sharyn Freant** God is good all the time. TY
February 12 at 7:10am · Like · 👍3

**Teresa Milner** TY GOD SOMEONE HAS A HEART THAT WAS NEAR THIS NEEDFUL YOUNG LADY THAT NEEDED SOMEONE AND WAS MADE FUN OF AND DOUBTED TY SO MUCH WHO EVER HELPED HER GOD WILL REPAY U AS I KNO HE ALREADY HAS BY BEING NAILED TO THE CROSS FOR EACH AND EVERYONE ONE OF US WHO EXCEPT HIM AMEN
February 12 at 7:44am · Like · 👍2

▮▮▮ est had been wonderful and mom is doing ▮▮▮ t that Marta and the shuttle to Northside are both closed. I'm going to be calling the hospital next to see if the security staff may have a 4x4 to bring us to the hospital when ▮▮▮ gets up and is ready.
February 12 at 8:35am · Like · 👍2

One of the most compelling stories from Snow Storm 2 involved Kelli Rochester and her family of 6 children, including three children with special needs. A tree had fallen on her house and had brought power lines on to her roof and she was, quite understandably, "freaking" out when the power kept flickering on and off and sparks kept flying from her roof. She had called 911 and her power company many times to no avail. Sometimes it was not possible to get through, and when she did, 911 told her to call the power company. The power company personnel were too busy to help her.

Kelli's first post was at 6:38 p.m. At first all we could offer was emotional support, but after 3 hours of terror for Kelli and her children, at 9:19 p.m., I decided I had to do something drastic to help in this situation.

**Kelli Rochester**

im in west georgia....a tree fell on my home a few minutes ago...thankfully it didnt go thru the roof...power is flickering off and on....i have 6 children here.....needless to say im very nervous right now...

Like · Comment · February 12 at 6:38pm near Carrollton, GA

👍 12 people like this.

💬 View previous comments                                    100 of 249

 **Maryann Day** How are you doing Kelli.. Are lights still flickering or has that settled down?
February 12 at 9:18pm · Like

 **Michelle Sollicito** Ok I am done with this. I am calling some major people to get you help
February 12 at 9:19pm · Like · 👍2

 **Kelli Rochester** it flickers when the wind blows...but not on a regular basis and my neighbor is letting me know when hes is acting up....im so tired...i want to cry...i just want this over....im physically and mentally exhausted!
February 12 at 9:19pm · Like

 **Kelli Rochester** carroll emc just keeps saying they will get here when they can.....
February 12 at 9:21pm · Like

 **Michelle Sollicito** kelli
February 12 at 9:22pm · Like

 **Maryann Day** Thanks Michelle Hang in there Kelli. I know I keep saying that and your really do not have much of a choice, but I feel so helpless . I'm in Lawrenceville .. I so wish I could get to you and just bring you somewhere safe. 😐 Right now you hang in there and when its all over and your kids are asleep you have your breakdown.. 😊 hugs sweetheart
February 12 at 9:23pm · Like

 **Michelle Sollicito** i have gema on the phone
February 12 at 9:23pm · Like

 **Michelle Sollicito** kelli
February 12 at 9:23pm · Like

 **Michelle Sollicito** give me ur number
February 12 at 9:23pm · Like

 **Kelli Rochester** ty so much
February 12 at 9:23pm · Like

 **Michelle Sollicito** gema on the case
February 12 at 9:25pm · Like · 👍1

 **Michelle Sollicito** they will call you kelli
February 12 at 9:25pm · Like

 **Kelli Rochester** ty so much!!!!
February 12 at 9:25pm · Like

 **Kelli Rochester** got the phone right here...

GEMA, to their credit, took my call extremely seriously and immediately helped Kelli.

**Kelli Rochester** talking to gema now ty ty ty
February 12 at 9:44pm · Like · 👍5

**Kelli Rochester** they are sending fire dept here...ty
February 12 at 9:46pm · Like · 👍4

It was so good to see a happy ending to this one.

**Kelli Rochester** yes they came and cant cut it away from the house because its private property. we were told to sleep in the basement,cut the power to the upstairs. call emc back and tell them the fire dept had been here and its about to take out all the lines. emc will cut it away.
February 12 at 10:19pm · Like · 👍2

**Kelli Rochester** going to cut those breakers off now...i mean shut
February 12 at 10:19pm · Like · 👍3

**Jude Matalavage** Good luck and stay safe.
February 12 at 10:20pm · Like

**Cabrino Ray** Sorry!! be safe.Try not to worry.
February 12 at 10:23pm · Like

**Kelli Rochester** i feel better knowing we can atleast stay here thru the night...tomorrow i can do more. im moving my kids matresses down to the basement.
February 12 at 10:24pm · Like · 👍2

**Kelli Rochester** i feel better...when i walked back in my baby girl said "are we safe?" and i smiled and said yes...so this has helped her as well. calling emc back and telling them what the fire dept. said
February 12 at 10:25pm · Like · 👍4

I later got this summary from Kelli of the whole experience from her perspective, in her own words:

From Kelli Rochester: i spent hours waiting on my emc to show up to remove the debris that had fallen on my roof.completely glued to snowedoutatlanta on my computer. my kids were scared and i couldn't console them for nothing!!! the power flickered on and off.after making several calls to my emc and 911.....michelle,the creator of snowedoutatlanta was kind enough to make some phone calls and within an hour,the fire trucks showed up and told me to cut the breakers off to the upstairs.it was the first time i was able to see some relief on my childrens faces....i remember my baby girl asking" are we safe now?" i told her "yes"...i moved their beds downstairs so they would not be in the rooms affected by the tree debris on the roof....very scarey time for us...between the help michelle gave us in making some calls and the people on snowedoutatlanta offering me support and talking to me and assuring me we would be okay.......thats what got me through that whole mess.

Other pleas for help were easier to resolve in Snow Storm 2 because we had a lot of resources within the group by then – Laura George (an amazing advocate for those with disabilities and their caregivers, especially in disasters), Lisa Matheson (Red Cross) and Tish Hammonds (Emergency Operations Center in Cobb and Douglas) were all helping us.

**Tiffany Bolick Hughes**

My husband's stepfather is on oxygen. He and my mother in law live in Riverdale. Their power has been out since 8 am. My MIL can't get through to GA Power to tell them that the power outrage prevents him from using the oxygen. His portable bottle will only last through tomorrow. Any suggestions/recommendations about what to do to get the power back on or more portable oxygen? Thanks!

Like · Comment · February 12 at 3:14pm

👍 7 people like this.

💬 View previous comments                    50 of 102

**Tiffany Bolick Hughes** I really appreciate everyone's help with this!!
February 12 at 3:53pm · Like · 👍 2

**Sam Stephen** Call 911 that's a life or death situation
February 12 at 3:54pm · Like · 👍 1

**Michelle Sollicito** Laura George and Lisa Matheson (Red Cross) are on the case - this will be resolved very soon - these girls are AWESOME!
February 12 at 3:55pm · Edited · Like · 👍 13

Laura and Lisa helped in this case and the issue was "resolved" shortly afterwards.

Tish Hammonds (Leticia Marsh, Deputy Director, Cobb and Douglas Public Health's Center for Emergency Preparedness and Response, in her non Facebook life) helped us to save a grandmother who was being kept alive by machines around her bed - until the power went out.

The first I knew of the problem was a post by Sheri Carter Carbone, but apparently she had seen it on a Fox 5 News website:

**Sheri Carter Carbone**

Someone posted this on another site not sure if anyone is close I was trying to get help to my grandmother whose stuck in a hospital bed at my aunt's house with no power none of her machines are working do to the power outage at

Please help my aunt get the power back on

Like · Comment · February 12 at 2:50pm

👍 5 people like this.

 **Elyse Nedrow** bump
February 12 at 2:51pm · Like

 **Jennifer Schmidt** Bump
February 12 at 2:52pm · Like

 **Heather Potts** bump
February 12 at 2:52pm · Like

 **Terri Sharpe** bump
February 12 at 2:53pm · Like

 **Brian Crystal Stewart** Sheri Carter Carbone please be careful posting addresses to the general public! Although most want to help, you just need to be careful! Hope someone can help you!
February 12 at 2:54pm · Like · 👍3

 **Stephanie Gurley Powell** Call 911. They will transport to hospital so that she is safe. Alsi, need to register with your power company that you have medical needs, they will prioritize you to the top. Most importantly, call 911 if needed.
February 12 at 2:55pm · Like · 👍2

 **Maria Clinkenbeard Cochran** You need a generator.. maybe someone had a generator they can borrow to keep her machines on
February 12 at 2:55pm · Like

 **Michelle Sollicito** Sheri Carter Carbone - please contact Tish Imstillstanding Hammonds she can help you
February 12 at 2:55pm · Like

 **Sheri Carter Carbone** It's not for me someone had posted on another site regarding his aunt so I put it on here for him. They would have to know the address to help and he put the address on the original post

So I responded to the original post on the Fox5Atlanta website and put Trent in touch with the EOC for Cobb County (Tish Hammonds)

**Trent Redmon** I was trying to get help to my grandmother whose stuck in a hospital bed at my aunt's house with no power none of her machines are working do to the power outage at

Please help my aunt get the power back on
Like · Reply · 👍 22 · February 12 at 2:46pm

 **Deanne L. McKimmey** You really need to all 911. If the roads allow it, EMS could come, check on her and provide her with medical care if needed. You could also tell the 911 operator what you just told us. Good Luck!!
Like · 👍 2 · February 12 at 3:00pm

 **Michelle Sollicito** If 911 doesnt work out contact Tish Imstillstanding Hammonds - she can help her cos it is Woodstock - she is in the EOC for Cobb county
Like · 👍 3 · February 12 at 3:02pm

 **Michelle Sollicito** Trent please contact to let me know if you still need help - the EOC in Cobb county is standing by to send someone
Like · 👍 3 · February 12 at 3:08pm

 **Michelle Sollicito** Sheri Carter Carbone - please send me the link or the name of the person who posted?
February 12 at 2:58pm · Like · 👍 1

 **Allison Carney** Bump
February 12 at 2:58pm · Like

 **Michelle Sollicito** Trent Redmond is the guy's name who posted this - I am adding this here so the EOC people can see it - they can get help to the woman
February 12 at 3:01pm · Like · 👍 2

 **Eden Barnett Nastal** Call 911
February 12 at 3:02pm · Like

 **Sheri Carter Carbone** https://www.facebook.com/Fox5atlanta /posts/297295000417927
February 12 at 3:02pm · Like · 👍 1

 **Trevor Williams** Here's contact for Woodstock Fire: ▅▅▅ ▅▅▅. They're 1.3 miles from that house. Also, the zip code for Woodstock is 30188, not 30296.
February 12 at 3:02pm · Like · 👍 1

 **Trevor Williams** Also, if she needs an ambulance, call 911. They'll get her one. All the ambulances in Cherokee have Humvee escorts right now.
February 12 at 3:03pm · Like · 👍 1

 **Michelle Sollicito** All is good - the deputy chief of the Emergency Operations Center in Cobb is on the line with them now sorting it out - that woman rocks!! Tish Imstillstanding Hammonds
February 12 at 3:32pm · Edited · Like · 👍 10

Within about 15 minutes of Tish getting involved, power trucks were at the house restoring power and a fire truck was there too:

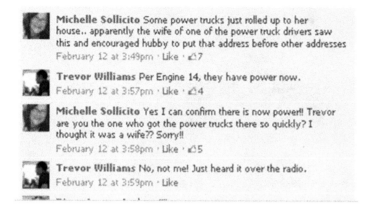

Michelle Sollicito Some power trucks just rolled up to her house.. apparently the wife of one of the power truck drivers saw this and encouraged hubby to put that address before other addresses
February 12 at 3:49pm · Like · 7

Trevor Williams Per Engine 14, they have power now.
February 12 at 3:57pm · Like · 4

Michelle Sollicito Yes I can confirm there is now power!! Trevor are you the one who got the power trucks there so quickly? I thought it was a wife?? Sorry!!
February 12 at 3:58pm · Like · 5

Trevor Williams No, not me! Just heard it over the radio.
February 12 at 3:59pm · Like

Apparently it was an amazing coincidence – the wife of the driver on the power truck was on our site and had told him to bump up the grandmother's location!

Some stories were more difficult to resolve, despite our attempts, like the one in which a pregnant lady needed help but no one could contact her because her power kept going out:

SamandMason Thompson

wheres the national guard guy ???? my friend is 8 months pregnant and has no power , shes in talking rock ga off tilley rd ....... the transformer blew earlier and the elect company came and fixed it and now it just blew again !!!! ....she was just in the hospital and they had to stop labor so im worried about her and she is a high risk pregnancy !

Like · Comment · February 12 at 11:04pm

👍 Yasemin Yalcinkaya and 7 others like this.

💬 View previous comments                                    50 of 84

Clinton Glenn Has she called 911, address, condition etc
February 13 at 12:16am · Like

Michelle Virginia Holland In talking rock, Ga off tilley rd is the only info in his post
February 13 at 12:17am · Like

Clinton Glenn Call [    ] if she needs further assistance
February 13 at 12:18am · Like · 1

Clinton Glenn I need confirmation before anything can be done if her friend calls we are on yhe way
February 13 at 12:20am · Like · 6

Yasemin Yalcinkaya Clinton, thanks for your help offer. I hope you guys can connect. I messaged her with your info also. If you hear from them, please let us know here.
February 13 at 12:27am · Like · 4

For hours we could not get any information, but then later there were some posts:

Holly McAllister Harrison Does anyone know if this lady is o.k.? Haven't heard from the poster in over 4 hours. Clinton was going to help, but couldn't get an answer.
February 13 at 3:40am · Like

**SamandMason Thompson** hey everyone ....i am so sorry i couldnt get back on here last night , rough night but my friend finally got power back on at 4am and she is okay but shes just nervous
February 13 at 7:47am · Like · 👍 4

 **SamandMason Thompson** thank you all so much for your concern and willingness to help her
February 13 at 7:47am · Like · 👍 1

 **SamandMason Thompson** hey everyone okay well her power is back off , ive messaged clinton .........my friend is cold and very uncomfortable
February 13 at 8:57am · Like

Again, despite numerous attempts to help her, there was silence for a while, but then another update..

 **SamandMason Thompson** hey , yes i posted 5 hours ago and she lost power and then we did again also and i cant get on here without wifi but they have fixed the power again and she is ok she was having pains but shes ok now and warm again
February 13 at 2:49pm · Like · 👍 3

 **SamandMason Thompson** thanks everyone , she had called me freaking out so i posted back to this and then boom the transformer blew again and lost power so i couldnt update
February 13 at 2:50pm · Like · 👍 2

Because no one could get any detailed information, all they could do was offer advice:

 **Deborah Joffre** SamandMason Thompson make sure your friend is drinking lots of fluids. Even slight dehydration when you are pregnant can bring on Braxton/hicks contraction.
February 13 at 3:20pm · Like · 👍 1

We were still helping people the next morning – including one guy having an allergic reaction who could not be helped by EMS as they were too busy, so in this case, Tish Hammonds (Leticia Mathis) this time asked *us* for help – she was working with the Cobb/Douglas Emergency Operations Center coordinators but was unable to get EMS to help because they were too busy with emergency calls:

**Michelle Sollicito**

I need help for a guy in Douglasville who needs to get to the hospital. Th
Cobb Emergency Operations Center contacted me because the EMS
cannot get to him as they are on life threatening calls right now. If
anyone can help let me know. I contacted Georgia Jeepers and 4x4
Helping Atlanta already

Like · Comment · February 13 at 9:46am

👍 Yasemin Yalcinkaya and 21 others like this.

💬 View previous comments                                          50 of 89

 **Lorri Kissell**
February 13 at 10:08am · Like

 **Tish Imstillstanding Hammonds** or call me at
February 13 at 10:08am · Edited · Like · 👍 1

 **Yasemin Yalcinkaya** Jim Fielder

 **Jim Fielder**
🏠 From Charlotte, North Carolina

February 13 at 10:09am · Like · Remove Preview

 **Stephen Johnson** Also try

 **Tammy Baxter**

February 13 at 10:12am · Like · 👍 1 · Remove Preview

 **Chad Artimovich** National Guard?
February 13 at 10:12am · Like · 👍 1

 **Tish Imstillstanding Hammonds** Tina called me and is warming her
car now! Thanks Tina!!!
February 13 at 10:13am · Like · 👍 4

 **Michelle Sollicito** Tish Imstillstanding Hammonds says that Tina Shaw
is on her way - not sure if that is Tina Cowley or someone else, but it
seems someone is on this case. Let me know when he gets to the hospital
safely someone thanks
February 13 at 10:15am · Like · 👍 3

Five different people offered to go help this guy and in the end "Stephany's husband" took him to the hospital. The Emergency Operations Center was extremely grateful. It was just another amazing example of how SnowedOutAtlanta came together to help people.

# The Numbers

The Associated Press carried a very useful article on "the numbers" involved in Snow Storm 2:

ATLANTA (AP) — Here's a look by the numbers at how some agencies are responding to a storm that is supposed to bring snow, "catastrophic" ice and widespread power outages to Georgia, including the Atlanta metro area.

SNOW AND ICE: Quarter-inch to a half-inch of ice around Atlanta and east. 6 to 10 inches of snow in north Georgia.

DEATHS: One storm-related death was reported in Georgia. Gov. Nathan Deal said a 50-year-old man in Butts County, about 45 miles southeast of Atlanta, died after he apparently slipped on ice outside his home.

POWER OUTAGES: More than 230,000 homes and businesses statewide were without electricity late Wednesday afternoon, up from 200,000 earlier in the day. Georgia Power and the Georgia Electric Membership Corp. said they were able to quickly restore power to thousands.

ROAD WRECKS: 251 crashes reported to the Georgia State Patrol between 2 a.m. and 9 p.m. Wednesday. 32 people injured on the roads, none killed.

THE ARMY NATIONAL GUARD: 1,000 guardsmen mobilized. 150 four-wheel drive vehicles, including Humvees.

EQUIPMENT: 705 pieces from Georgia Department of Transportation, including trucks, plows, salt spreaders. 125 spreaders and snow plows in city of Atlanta.

STAFF: 2,130 state transportation workers on call.

SALT AND GRAVEL: 41,953 tons of gravel and 22,199 tons of salt stockpiled for use statewide, and Georgia Department of Transportation expects to get more. 3,000 tons for city of Atlanta roads.

UTILITIES: 200 trucks from throughout the Southeast available to start restoring power.

WARMING SHELTERS: At least 57 statewide including 35 National Guard armories and 11 Georgia state parks with 2,800 cots available. Shelters also opened at some police precincts, fire stations, churches and recreation centers in metro Atlanta.

FLIGHTS: 1,643 flights to and from Atlanta's airport canceled Wednesday and an additional 664 Thursday flights canceled, according to the website FlightAware. 100,000 gallons of de-icing fluid, 100,000 pounds of de-icing pellets, salt and sand for runways.

LAST TIME: In 2000, an ice storm in the Atlanta area left more than 500,000 homes and businesses without power. Damages topped $35 million. A storm in 1973 caused an estimated 200,000 homes and businesses to lose power.

## Spinoff Groups

Two groups that deserve a special mention are the "GeorgiaJeepers" Facebook group and the "4x4 Helping Atlanta" Facebook group. They each helped a great deal in the first snowstorm, but they were also invaluable in the second.

In fact the 4x4's Helping Atlanta group was one of many groups that grew directly out of SnowedOutAtlanta, in this case, as a direct result of this post:

**Mark Lowery**
To all the men that have Jeeps are 4 X 4.. with gas.. I think we should do something..
Like · Comment · January 29 at 12:40am

Here, Stephen Johnson tells the story of how 4x4's Helping Atlanta got started:

**Stephen Johnson**
Mark had made a post on your group saying he thought guys with 4x4s should go out and help people and I responded saying I was thinking about making a group for people with 4x4s that might be able to help in the morning and he told me he was ready to go out that night and start helping so I went ahead and made the group and we worked through the night trying to organize and people with 4x4s who wanted to help and hooking them up with people who were posting in your group that needed help.

Often, people found out about these groups through SnowedOutAtlanta but went on to the other groups either to offer help or to get help

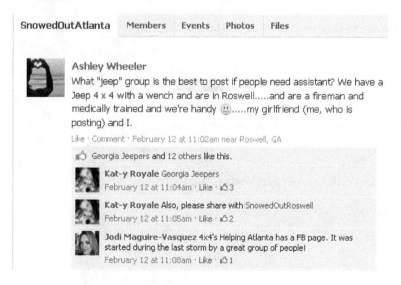

Sometimes SnowedOutAtlanta worked in conjunction with 4x4's Helping Atlanta to get people home, like in this case where 4x4 members were on their way to help Steven Taylor, but SnowedOutAtlanta meanwhile got him a lift home from someone at the hospital.

**4x4's Helping Atlanta**      Members      Events      Photos      Files

**Steven Taylor**
Been stranded since being released at 11 PM at Wellstar Cobb Hospital. I have a one year old daughter at home having fits without her Daddy. I live approx 4 miles from the hospital near the intersection of Austell Rd and Cunningham Rd. Any available help would be greatly appreciated.

Unlike · Comment · Share · February 13 at 8:23am

👍 You, Yasemin Yalcinkaya and Debbie Allen like this.

> **Michelle Sollicito** are you the same guy from SnowedOutAtlanta? I was about to post about you if so.. do not want to duplicate! 😊
> February 13 at 8:33am · Like · 👍 1

> **Gregory Phillips** Will be headed that way in a few minutes.
> February 13 at 8:35am · Like · 👍 3

> **Steven Taylor** Much obliged sir
> February 13 at 8:37am · Like · 👍 1

> **Gregory Phillips** Np en route
> February 13 at 8:39am · Like · 👍 1

> **Jon Dean** Anyone on the way yet?
> February 13 at 8:41am · Like

> **Jon Dean** Sorry Gregory Phillips I couldn't see the comments.
> February 13 at 8:41am · Like

> **Gregory Phillips** Np
> February 13 at 8:53am · Like

> **Gregory Phillips** He got a ride from hospital staff so should be good. Didn't make it in time. Lol
> February 13 at 8:58am · Like · 👍 3

> **Andre Anderson** I'm not far from there. Call or text. ▬▬▬▬▬
> February 13 at 9:04am · Like · 👍 1

> **Steven Taylor** I made it home safe. Thank you to everyone that was willing to reach out and help.
> February 13 at 9:19am · Like · 👍 2

> **Gregory Phillips** He got a ride Andre Anderson was headed there but someone offered from the hospital.
> February 13 at 9:20am · Like · 👍 1

Many other amazing groups grew out of the wonderful spirit created by SnowedOutAtlanta (none of which were created by me).

Because we wanted to reduce the bandwidth in SnowedOutAtlanta group by not posting thank yous there, many "Thank You" groups sprang up to say thank you to those who had helped during the storm.

Thank You Atlanta, Ga SnowApocalypse 2014 and SnowedOutAtlanta-Thanks and Rescue Stories are just two I remember.  There were countless others.  Many had offers of gifts, massages and other thanks for those who had helped.

"Pay It Forward – Atlanta" was an attempt to carry forward the spirit from SnowedOutAtlanta, fostering a spirit of community and a spirit of helping others.

# Chapter 3 – Social Media - Why it Did/Did Not Work

## Online Groups/Communities

I have a long history in computing. I got my first home computer (a Sinclair ZX Spectrum) when I was 11 years old, in 1979. I wrote computer games in machine code before I went to university. I obtained my degree in Business Computing Systems in 1990, having decided to be an IT Consultant. I have spent 25 years working in the computing industry as an IT Consultant – for various companies such as Accenture (then Andersen Consulting), Sema (now Schlumberger), Cap Gemini, Yahoo! and Earthlink, amongst others.

[Warning! This is the techy bit!]

I have written desktop applications (for those geeks reading this – I started in C/Unix/Oracle with X/Motif and moved on to Visual Basic 3 and Visual C++ with Sybase and SQL Server), designed and built databases from scratch and, of course, built many websites, including the technical architecture that supports eBusiness transactions behind the scenes for websites to interact with ebay, Amazon, Facebook, Google and Yahoo! via "APIs" (application programming interfaces). Again, for the geeks, I know C# and .Net really well and am Microsoft certified many times over (currently MCTS and MCP) as well as certified by ODesk and Brainbench in a wide range of technologies (including HTML, SQL Server, XML, Javascript, Network Security, Internet Security, Ecommerce). I have run a number of large projects involving putting many technologies together, with teams spreading across the world in some cases.

[End of techy bit!]

So I know a bit about computing!

Most recently, I have been concentrating on my own business, TxtToAd.com, which is a bit like ebay or Craigslist, but allows people to post ads and view ads using Facebook (ads are posted via the Facebook API).

So I know a lot about how Facebook works, behind the scenes too.

And, of course, I have also run many Facebook pages and groups, mainly aimed at moms with children or those interested in local education issues in Marietta where I live. Before SnowedOutAtlanta, MariettaMoms was the main Facebook group I ran.

Marietta Moms is my mom's group in the "real world." It has evolved over 7 years. When I first started, it, like SnowedOutAtlanta, grew very fast too – at that time, we were using Meetup.com to host it and it grew so fast I felt uncomfortable with its size – 700 members at one time! It was difficult to manage 700 members while trying to reduce negativity and also trying hard not to charge money for the service. When I started Marietta Moms I had resolved never to charge money for running it as I wanted it to be available to single moms / moms on low incomes who might feel excluded.

However, as the group got so large, I was paying huge hosting fees for the group, and members persuaded me to charge a small fee to recoup those losses. Although I begrudgingly gave in and charged those fees I was never happy about it and in the end, my "co-admins" and I could not agree on how to manage such a large group because I did not want to make any kind of profit over and above the hosting costs, and so the co-admins split off and started another mom's group instead. I felt much more comfortable with a smaller group, charging no fees.

It is quite ironic now that 700 members made me so uncomfortable, given that I most recently managed a "small town" of 55,000 people online through one of the worst crises any mayor or governor has ever had to manage a group of people through, with quite a high degree of success. Of course, if anyone had asked me beforehand, to do it, I would have laughed and of course, refused! But thrust into that situation, I felt I had to continue to ensure no lives were lost!

Meetup.com fees meant that I had to move my Marietta Moms group elsewhere so that I did not have to charge fees to my members. I knew my choice of group hosting platform could make a big difference to the success or otherwise of the mom's group.

Throughout the years I had used a number of "group platforms" – from Cix (probably the best groups platform I ever used, Cix was a community online service started in the UK in 1987 – see http://www.cixonline.com/– I was a member in the early 1990's) and its American rival from about the same time period, Compuserve (still around now – see http://webcenters.netscape.compuserve.com/menu/) through to AOL, Yahoo! Groups, Google Groups, Google+ etc.

Now I wanted to try the latest offerings in the group/social community field to be sure I was using the best free offering out there. For a while I moved the group to Yahoo! Groups just because I knew how to use the technology and had hosted lots of free groups on there in the past (plus, I had worked for Yahoo! and my husband still did!). But I knew that was a temporary home for the group.

I evaluated a number of offerings at that time and decided to move the group to Ning.com as it was so flexible and powerful. It had numerous great features and we all loved the site so much. However, after one year on that platform, Ning became too popular! It started to charge hosting fees because it *could*!

At first, I started evaluating alternative platforms but then Steve Worrall, an excellent family lawyer in our area, offered to pay the hosting costs for one year in a Sponsorship deal. I was so grateful as it meant we could stay on our platform of choice for one more year while I looked around for an alternative.

After one year, we moved to my next best choice which was Spruz.com. At the time Spruz.com was very like Ning.com but it had a lot of bugs. However, I was extremely impressed at how quickly they fixed all the bugs, because as more and more Ning.com groups moved over to Spruz.com, they had more money available to work on their platform. Of course, with great popularity, came hosting costs, so this time we moved to Facebook, simply because by then many of my members were already on it.

Although Facebook made it easy to connect with some members (those who were already on it) it meant we left a lot of people behind because a lot of members just did not like Facebook. Also, of course, Facebook groups simply did not have some of the great features that a platform like Ning or Spruz had available (the ability to add rss feeds, widgets etc. – see http://mariettamoms.spruz.com to see what I mean), but a group on Facebook was free, and it would make it easy to share information between us and to ensure that members got updates regularly. So we muddled through, and coped with the lack of features. I started many other Facebook groups and pages over the past few years also, including mainly Facebook pages related to education or related to my business TxtToAd.com.

During all my time managing groups and pages within Facebook, I had never experienced many "bugs," only a lack of features. Of course, SnowedOutAtlanta stretched Facebook to its limits – Facebook admitted they had never before experienced a group that grew as quickly, and that their technology was having trouble handling the speed of the growth involved. However, having worked in IT for so long, I know that the load it handled that night was exceptional and, given that load, Facebook stood up very well. As far as I know the site was never unavailable, even at peak times.

So, there were ways in which Facebook was perfect for SnowedOutAtlanta, enabling us to help so many people with no notice, and of course, we also had some issues. I want to highlight both in this chapter, as I hope to help others who run social media groups in the future, especially in the disaster relief/management fields. I also hope it will help Facebook to improve their product.

# Why Facebook *Did* Work

Having analyzed what happened in detail, with leading psychologists and social media experts, I have come up with a checklist of why Facebook worked that day and what lessons can be learned from the whole experience.

1. The Facebook Effect

Of course, the main reason Facebook worked for SnowedOutAtlanta was the sheer *speed* at which the group was able to grow. This phenomenon, known as the "The Facebook Effect"[ii], after the term was coined in the book by that name, has been experienced by Facebook pages and groups in the past but never at the velocity reached that first night by SnowedOutAtlanta. The more people invited to join the group, the more of their friends found out about the group, and so they joined the group, and so did their friends and so on, leading to an almost exponential join rate! I believe the *desperation* and *neediness* of many of the people who joined the group exacerbated that "join up rate" because it fulfilled a need at a critical time – the need both to get help, but also the need *to be of assistance* to others.

2. Facebook Groups

I strongly believe that a large factor in the success of SnowedOutAtlanta was the fact that it was housed in a Facebook *Group* rather than on a Facebook *Page*. Before I started the group I had a mental debate with myself about which I should create.

A Facebook Page, for me, is a good way to get information out to a lot of people. It is ideally suited to a situation where there is one person or organization (the "owner") which has all the information and everyone else is just reading it/consuming it. It is more like a "broadcast of information."

A Facebook Group is more like an *exchange* where lots of people in the group have information and can share it with others and where discussions do not necessarily involve the one person or organization (the "owner") who started the group. In this manner, a group is more like an "exchange of information."

I did not know for certain, but my gut feel told me when I started the group that this is what I needed – a group, and not a page. I felt that in many cases I would have to get out of conversations and let the people in need talk directly to the people who could help them without my involvement at all.

Little did I know how great a decision that would turn out to be. There is absolutely no way so many people could have been helped that night if I had made the decision to create a Page instead.

I cannot speak for every industry when I talk about how much more powerful Facebook groups are than Facebook pages. However, for someone who has worked within the Utility industry as an IT Consultant quite a bit over the years, I know the most important lesson learned from this experience for Utilities, should be that Facebook groups are very different to Facebook pages not only because they allow customers to *self-service* but because **groups change behavior**.

Utility companies have been trying to change consumer behavior by providing them with all kinds of information and tools for years, but have been frustrated to see only minor changes in consumer behavior as a result of a great deal of effort.

In two incidents – Snow Storm 1 and Snow Storm 2 – I saw much more direct behavior change as a result of the SnowedOutAtlanta group, where members were informing each other and helping each other to make decisions – than I have seen in years of looking at behavior change due to tools and charts.

Groups enable those who have information to share it with those who need it very quickly. They enable the information-givers to feel good about themselves because they have helped others and they make it much more likely that the information-receivers will *take action* in response to that information (change their behavior) because there is a two-way discussion (or more often, a multi-way discussion), clarifying issues and providing guidance. People feel supported in making decisions they make, and they feel that if they have further questions or issues they can return to the group for more support and assistance.

We saw this countless times during SnowedOutAtlanta's existence.

Of course, for utility companies (and, I am sure, for many other companies), it would be much cheaper to allow a group of customers to help one another than it is for the utility to pay a group of social media experts to sit and reply to each and every Facebook post (or tweet) from their customers – which, in turn, is cheaper than setting up a group of telephone operators or live chat operators to help customers - or an Interactive Voice Response system to help them to "self-service."

Because, in emergency situations, often the customers would have more information between them than the utility itself, customers in a Facebook group would often self-service in providing facts, dispelling rumors and shaping perceptions about the situation between them. As a result, I have recommended to the utility companies that they employ Facebook groups to enable and empower their customers to self-service and help one another.

**Joe Gilliom**

Georgia Power does not provide service to all counties. This map shows number outages for the entire state by region. Not a interactive map, but give you the big picture. UnityinDisasters.org has links and infor state on our home page.

**Current Outages By Region**
georgiaemc.com

Like · Comment · Share · February 12 at 1:19pm

👍 Corazon Javier Ketchem likes this.

Write a comment...

Although, of course, there is a danger that the perception being shaped within a group is an erroneous one. But my belief, as a direct result of my experience with SnowedOutAtlanta, is that in general, if an erroneous perception is being built up, it is knocked down pretty quickly by others in the group. Those who have "evidence" that the perception is wrong tend to provide that evidence to counteract the errant perception. Group dynamics are very powerful in enabling the "truth" to rise to the top.

For example, early on in Snow Storm 2, SnowedOutAtlanta group members expressed fears that the utility companies might not be prepared for huge outages. Those fears were quickly knocked down by a number of members who posted evidence that the utilities were indeed very well prepared:

**Daniel Twin**

Georgia Power ready for this snow storm at White Water Marietta Ga

**Kristin Egolinsky**
Just a bit of "good" news for y'all. Our largest Electric/utility Company in Michigan has just sent out the call and line workers, engineers & field managers are gearing up and preparing to come help restore power - should the worst happen. I'm sure that other companies across the country are doing the same. (But I don't have 1st hand knowledge of them.)
Especially now that FEMA (yes, the federal branch) has also declared S.O.E. In Georgia...

Like · Comment · February 11 at 2:38pm

👍 51 people like this.

 **Stacy Grill Maher** Yay for my home state!
February 11 at 2:44pm · Like · 👍2

 **Wenyan Yuan** Thank you!!!
February 11 at 2:51pm · Like

 **Rebel Wilson** Great just want I wanted to read that Georgia is sending out S.O.E. since I live here.
February 11 at 2:55pm · Like

 **Ruth Zackowitz Hartman** I also know FPL from Florida is on their way, too....
February 11 at 3:05pm · Like · 👍1

Perception is more important than reality on social media. For example, before Snow Storm 2, people felt very aware of the dangers to be posed by the oncoming storm. There was a unified message from the governor, GEMA, the police departments, and all the local EMAs that made it very clear that this storm could be very serious and people heeded those warnings.

People in the group seemed to feel very happy with the utility companies because they felt informed and prepared for the outages to come. "Power users" on the SnowedOutAtlanta site posted useful information and helped everyone stay aware of what was going on at all times.

Facebook groups are also different to Facebook pages because of the unique way in which they make inherent use of group dynamics. I noticed during SnowedOutAtlanta how quickly people learned to "bump" the most critical cases by either "liking" the post or commenting on the post in a kind of voting system that enabled the most needy cases to bubble to the top and get the most attention.

I noticed also how psychologically important it was for those in need to feel part of a group consisting of so many people – the terror of being alone and cold in a car knowing that no emergency services could reach people was replaced with a feeling of support, help, information and – yes, love - from members of SnowedOutAtlanta. Panic subsided as people joined the group and received responses, options and information.

The group empowered people to help themselves and help others and that was not only practically important, in allowing people to be rescued, but also psychologically important, in helping them get through a crisis.

3. Responsiveness

I believe that another reason that Facebook was such a great platform to support the success of SnowedOutAtlanta was because it was not only available on most devices – computers, smartphones and tablets, but it performed *really well* on all of them.

Members were accessing SnowedOutAtlanta using a wide range of devices and the fact that even the Facebook app continued to work on most smartphones even throughout the most intense use of the group is a great credit to Facebook.

Having written a few apps for smartphones I know how difficult it is to write them. It is especially difficult to write them in such a way that they stand up to intense load. So, the fact that the mobile apps worked right through the night of both snowstorms seems almost miraculous to me and Facebook should be hailed for such an achievement. There were delays and difficulties using the apps – members had to trawl through so many posts to get to the one(s) relevant to them – but generally speaking, there was not much Facebook could have done better in supporting mobile users throughout this experience.

I do not know the percentage of users who were accessing the site using mobile devices, but I do know it was pretty high, because many of those stranded had only their smartphones available. I also know that during the peak times - when the site was being used by 30-40,000 people all at the same time! – and when posts were coming in at a rate of 100s per minute – both the main Facebook site and the mobile versions all continued to respond. They were slow at times but they still responded.

4. Central Source of Great Information

The "Pinned Post" was central to the success of SnowedOutAtlanta. Having one post which everyone could always see at the top of the page in the group, containing the most up-to-date information on a number of topics, was crucial in helping so many people. Only admins could modify the post, so that information was not deleted by accident, but it was updated regularly with new phone numbers, websites, shelter locations, Google map urls, tips for survival, outage tips etc. Without the pinned post, many of the would-be helpers would not have been able to assist so many people.

## Facebook Issues

Just around midnight during Snow Storm 1, I started to notice that the Facebook group's response time was getting worse as more and more members joined the group. It seemed that at around 29,000 members, with around 100 posts per minute, we hit a turning point. It was becoming difficult to use the group as the site was taking a long time to respond to requests, notifications were taking over the screen because there were such a huge number of them and it was even more difficult for me to approve the huge number of requests to join coming in at a rate of 300 every 15 minutes.

The problems continued, and Facebook had a lot of trouble keeping up. I realized I needed to reduce the load on the main site somehow. I realized that I also needed to make it easier for many people to find help in the location they were in. I wondered if I could "kill two birds with one stone" by creating sub-groups aligned to these locations.

I thought about the possibilities and the problems that could come from such a change right in the middle of all that was going on. It was a big risk - I knew it would take me some time to create these groups, and I was even more worried about how long it might take to migrate people to those new groups.

But I went ahead and started to create sub-groups.

Because I realized that a great number of the members in SnowedOutAtlanta were actually from the area in which I lived (East Cobb) due to the infamous "six degrees of separation rule" (often used to describe Facebook growth and relationships), and because I started the group, I created a special sub-group called SnowedOutEastCobb to cater for those in my area.

Then I created sub-groups for the four main areas of Atlanta: SnowedOutNorthAtlanta, SnowedOutSouthAtlanta, SnowedOutWestAtlanta and SnowedOutEastAtlanta.

I started to communicate to all SnowedOutAtlanta members that they should join these sub-groups and as soon as I did so, *these groups* started to grow at a phenomenal rate immediately also. For people on cellphones with limited battery life, trawling through the huge amount of content on the main group was too much, and these sub-groups were a welcome alternative.

The sub-groups became so popular that other people started to create further sub-groups, some with my help and some without. For all the sub-groups I created, I tried to ensure that I kept the same "Pinned Post" up-to-date in each one so that they all had access to the latest information. Creating and managing so many sub-groups was no small task logistically but it certainly helped the main group's response times considerably and helped those on cellphones find help much more easily than they had before.

When others asked for permission to create other sub-groups along the same lines I generally said "yes." I knew I could not prevent them from creating more sub-groups, though I was anxious that having too many groups might dilute the usefulness of the sub-groups in helping people. I said "yes" to some groups that appeared to make sense to me, but "no" to others that I felt might dilute the groups' helpfulness (especially where I felt a new sub-group would duplicate an old sub-group).  The groups I endorsed received the "official pinned post" but the others did not, and that was the only way I could think of to indicate which sub-groups were "official" at that time – later we added a common photo to the top of all the groups also.

I posted on the main group that the site was not able to cope, and asked people to instead post in the sub-groups.  I was amazed at how quickly people followed that instruction!  Very quickly the main site was operating and responding well again, and the sub-groups were more effective at helping people anyway so it turned out really well.

I posted the urls of the new sub-groups in the pinned post on the main site, and in all the sub-groups, so that new members of the main site would also find out quickly about the sub-groups and would move there.  For a while all I was doing was approving member requests to join either the main group or the sub-groups.  It was pretty hectic for some time.

Just after I had created all the sub-groups, while the main group was still experiencing extremely high load, Facebook contacted me at 3 a.m. on January 29 about SnowedOutAtlanta.  Allie Townsend is the managing editor at Facebook:

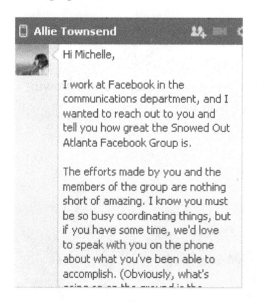

I mentioned the fact that under the extreme load, the site was responding very slowly.  I also told her about a weird "bug" I was experiencing on the site – the search engine for members was finding some members but not finding others.  Allie confirmed that the problems I was having were probably related to the rapid growth rate of the group.

Facebook tried really hard to resolve the problems but it seemed that the rapid growth of the group left a number of issues that were not easy to resolve.

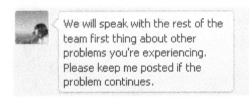

Allie confirmed that the group was growing at an unprecedented rate and that, because of the growth rate, we were experiencing bugs that had probably never been seen before.

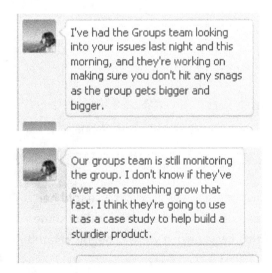

Over the lifetime of the group, we experienced a number of issues caused by the growth rate of the group – these included problems with searching for both posts and members. Some posts and members could be found, while others could not. Because we could not find some members we could not do things such as make them admins, or block them or ban them. To add to the confusion, the members we *could* find, it seemed, would sometimes find they had been "banned" even though the admins had only "removed" them from the group, due to another bug.

A number of members who had also run other Facebook groups did not believe that the problems I was reporting were really happening, so I invited a few people to try being admins and try to help me fix the problem. However, all of them, even the most experienced, eventually admitted the problems were caused by "Facebook bugs."

Of course, all websites have "bugs." These bugs were much more visible than they might otherwise have been because 50,000 people were watching. But I do not want that to reflect badly on Facebook.

As an IT consultant with 25+ years' experience, I have never seen a website take quite as much "update load" as Facebook did that night on the SnowedOutAtlanta group. "Update load" (whereby information is being "posted" to a website) is very different to "view load"(whereby users are simply looking at content on a website) – many websites handle huge quantities of views every day, but handling huge quantities of updates is very much more difficult because of the stress it puts on the database supporting the website. Given the huge "update load," I was amazed that the site did not fall over completely. At no point in its life was SnowedOutAtlanta "unavailable" to my knowledge, and for that, the Facebook team should be extremely proud, in my opinion.

[Warning! The techy bit!]

For the techies reading this, I believe that Facebook is written mainly in php with mysql database at the back end so it is extremely impressive how the site held up against 50,000 people accessing it almost simultaneously, not just viewing the website, but most of the time inserting/updating it also. Even in stress testing of huge websites (testing in which I have been purposely trying to make a website fall over due to overload) I have never seen a website stand up so well to such extreme usage. So I take my hat off to Facebook for that. The "bugs" were annoying and sometimes embarrassing and frustrating, but they were by far so much better than the alternative: for the site to have been inaccessible at peak "need" time.

[end of techy bit]

To their credit, Facebook asked for feedback on key things they could do to improve the experience in the group so I sent them a "Top 10 list" a day or two after Snow Storm 1 listing these:

1. Summary
   This document is a list of suggestions of technical changes to Groups on Facebook that I believe would be useful in future Disaster Relief situations. Many of them would be useful in general for Groups users also.

2. Search Engine
   By far the most important change I would suggest is to add a real Search Engine. It is very important in Disaster Relief to be able to find other posts that have been posted that provide important information. It was very frustrating to know that you saw some crucial info but it had disappeared off the page and it was so difficult to find it again. I think the "leaf" element being shown in the results of a search is part of the problem.. because the leaf is the top level post

whereas I think the leaf should be the comment if the key phrase is found in the comment (with a summary of the top level post above the comment maybe).

3.  Settings
    It would be really useful in Disaster Relief situations (where the speed element is of great importance) if there was a "public group" setting which allowed anyone to join without needing any approval at all. I spent most of Tuesday night simply clicking on the "Approve All" button because so many people were joining every time I refreshed the approval page there were more to approve! I could have spent more of my time actually finding info and helping people if I did not have to do that. I was so scared not to approve people quickly in case they were in real need – if they were in danger of dying or something, so I made it a point to keep approving any member requests as soon as I could. I had the settings set so that people were supposed to be able to invite their friends but everyone told me they could not do that or it was not working. I set the group to the most open settings possible.

4.  Members Search
    It seemed that once we hit around 20,000 members it was impossible to search for some members (possibly the oldest members in the group, not sure). In the members page I would type in their names and it would come up not found. Once Allie told me this was due to the size of the group I created smaller groups and told people to join those and they did – and those groups functioned fine. She was looking into resolving this issue but I am not sure if it is resolved yet.

5.  Size of Group
    When the group was the busiest (3-5am Weds morning) response times were VERY SLOW on the group. I know there were thousands of posts, and I know how difficult it is to manage that kind of load coming in so am not sure if that can be improved but wanted to mention it. I am guessing though, that requests to a particular group all go to the same server on the Facebook server farm right now? Is that correct? If so, maybe load could be spread across many servers? If not, then maybe put posts in a separate database server to the comments so that the load can be spread at the database layer? Approving members was particularly slow, see below.

6.  Approving Members
    Once the group grew large, approving members was problematic. I think it was because new member requests would come in while Facebook was still trying to process an Approve All and maybe there was not a database snapshot/lock out so that when it started the Approve All there would be say 300 members to approve but by the time all those members were processed, another 25 requests for Approval would come in and the process would get confused. It would appear as though about half of the people had been approved and then the Facebook page would either freeze or come up with a new number of people to Approve All for and say "confirm?"

7.  Shared Documents
    I had to resort to using Google Docs because we could not get Facebook shared docs to work effectively in that environment. We needed many people to be able to edit a document at the same time and that did not seem possible with Facebook shared files/docs. Uploading a new version would overwrite changes someone else was uploading so we used Google Docs instead. I wish Facebook had a Shared Docs that worked like Google Docs. Shared docs are crucial to managing an environment like this because people need to be able to add new info in real time to a list of info.

8.  Admin Permissions
    I wish it was possible to give someone permission to be an admin but then limit what they can do with that in some ways. Some of my admins got power crazy while I was asleep. They were banning people and inviting other people to be admins. I would have liked to prevent them from adding other admins and prevent them from banning people.

9.  Notifications
    I am not sure if this is my ignorance but I think there were a number of issues with Notifications.

a)  I got an email for every single person who tried to join the group, every single post / comment etc. it seemed too. Yahoo! Mail could not cope and I could not get into my email as a result!! My husband works for Yahoo! and I used to work at Yahoo! so this is embarrassing to admit ;-)

b)  I had complaints that people who had turned off notifications were still getting notifications and that even people who had left the group were still getting notifications. This happened for a lot of people so I think it was true. Allie knew about it and I thought she had resolved it but I am still getting complaints from some people. This may be related to the size of the group.

10. Sub-groups

It would be nice to have a concept of sub-groups. My SnowedOutAtlanta group had sub-groups SnowedOutSouthAtlanta and SnowedOutNorthAtlanta etc. but the only way I knew to get people to them was by putting links to them in the pinned post. It would be nice if you could make sub-groups of the main group but I am sure that would be technically complex (e.g. if you resign from the main group would you still be a member of the sub-group and would notifications work for both or either).

Another issue we experienced with Facebook related to "personality issues." Many people have reminded me that I was managing "a small town online" (50,000 people), through two of the worst crises any governor or mayor ever had to manage such a huge group of people through.

Whenever anyone manages so many people, especially through a stressful period created by a crisis, one expects to experience personality issues.

During Snow Storm 1, I was quite amazed at how few of these issues showed themselves. I had what I believed to be a minor issue caused by one or many admins who were helping me to run the sites while I was asleep (at that point I had not slept for 36 hours, and even then I only had a nap for four hours, but during this time, some trouble occurred). One or many of the admins got a little "power crazy" and upset a few people but I had no idea which admin was involved, so I simply removed the admins who had been helping during that time period, and the problem was seemingly nipped in the bud. This seemed to be the only real problem during Snow Storm 1.

After Snow Storm 1, I was looking out for the inevitable negativity to come creeping into the group after the crisis had died down - especially as people who had not been involved in the crisis itself came on board - and as soon as it did, I shut down the group. The crisis was over at that time and a lot of people had nothing else to do because they were snowbound inside their homes, so it was inevitable that negativity would creep in. I did not want it to detract from the wonderful spirit that had been created.

Looking back, I should have done the same after Snow Storm 2, but I caved to pressure from those who wanted to keep the group open. Because I left it open, there was an influx of negativity which really spoiled the ethos of the group. If I could have a "do over" probably the only thing I would do differently would be to close the group immediately after Snow Storm 2 was over.

One thing I learned from the negativity was that responding to those who post only negative comments is a waste of time and energy and actually simply makes their comments worse. It is like adding fuel to a fire.

Throughout SnowedOutAtlanta, I had a policy of not banning people from the group unless they made it impossible for the rest of us to help people because of their actions. I did not want to block someone and then later to find out that person needed help and could not access our group. Other admins who were helping me felt that was the wrong approach, and they banned a few people, which again added fuel to their fire.

Looking back I believe I should not have allowed those admins to ban anyone. It is simply best to educate members to use the great Facebook features that allow you to ignore those people – to either block or ignore them, turn off notifications on threads they are posting on, etc.

In general, there are some lessons learned from this whole experience of managing a large Facebook group through a crisis. All these tips are, in my opinion, good tips for managing any Facebook group, big or small:

- Ban no one
- Use only trusted people as admins
- Educate members on how to use Facebook tools to block or ignore people or threads if they do not like their posts
- Discourage members from replying to negative posts, so adding fuel to the fire
- Empower members of the group to self-serve and help others as much as possible
- Use shared documents and maps so that all members can access all information as much as possible
- Use a pinned post to accumulate information that most people in the group will need

# Chapter 4 – Psychology of It All

Linda Gunter, an expert in the Psychology of Disasters, wrote most of this chapter after discussing SnowedOutAtlanta with me. I want to thank Linda for all the brainstorming she did with me on the psychological implications of what happened on SnowedOutAtlanta and how it applies to other disasters too. She has been an invaluable source of information on this topic, of which I knew very little until I spoke to her.

Much of Linda's experience is from other disasters – such as the Fukushima earthquake/tsunami disaster in Japan – and yet, as you will see, it is very relevant to the SnowedOutAtlanta experience.

## Psychology – Disasters

A disaster scenario: the media have been broadcasting storm warnings for days, an approaching weather system may create hazardous conditions for your area. Once the storm hits, people are stranded on the highway, children remain at school, folks had to sleep in their office or business. Shelters opened, people find military style sleeping arrangements, no privacy and nutritious but basic food. With their immediate needs met, people want to know if other members of the family are safe? How can they take care of pets and their elderly neighbors? How can they locate the missing? Next the longer term issues become obtaining medications, prescription glasses, and finding a power outlet, an internet connection and maybe even access to a computer or phone. The lack of sleep and privacy and the noise grate on already frazzled nerves. There is very little to do but talk with other evacuees and share your worries and concerns. The lack of certainty about the safety of your family is bothersome, but the realization that some people are worse off keeps the complaining minimal. Some people may experience headaches, high blood pressure or depression. Decision making becomes problematic for many people, stress leads to confusion.

I spoke in detail to Linda about these symptoms that people experience during disasters. We are both strong believers in the mind-body connection. I saw time and time again during the lifetime of SnowedOutAtlanta, how the physical symptoms people experienced at first due to the stress and confusion of the situation subsided as soon as people felt supported and connected.

It is normal to continue to replay the situation in your mind over and over again – could you have done something different? Could you, should you be doing something different now? How best to cope with this nagging fear that things will never be right? There is sadness, possibly even grief that wells up and may feel overwhelming. How can you go on? You feel out of control. How can you deal with the uncertainty? How can you start to take control of your life?

Many people, who do not want to be identified, told me that they experienced panic attacks, PTSD-like symptoms, grief, and depression as a result of their experience during Snow Storm 1. They are reluctant to open up publicly about it due to the stigma associated with those symptoms and the ridicule some have seen others subject to since the storm. I believe these symptoms are very real, and I believe that some people in the snow storm were in great fear for their lives for a prolonged amount of time, so their experience of those symptoms is not a sign of weakness. Only others who experienced similar situations – sitting in a dark, cold car with no gas, with cars crashing and sliding across roads all around them – could understand what they went through.

We know that everyone experiences a natural disaster in his or her own way, it is difficult to predict whether people will be resilient, depressed or stressed from their individual circumstances. Medical researchers have begun to understand the brain-emotion-immune system interconnectedness. In a crisis situation, people naturally react to fear of the unknown. Biologically what happens is their system releases stress hormones, testosterone levels rise and a "fight or flight" reaction is triggered. An individual's education, previous experiences with a snow storm, for example, and genetic history, along with habits all factor into how we behave. The immediate experience—being stuck on the highway for example - is obviously stressful. It is also natural to want to punish and blame those "responsible" for the lack of preparation for a weather event. Some people experience more stress when they no longer have access to their normal/habitual solutions to an increase in their anxiety (cigarettes, alcohol, cleaning etc.) becoming more anxious and fearful. Coping mechanisms are as varied as our personalities, how much control we feel over our situation and the likelihood of a safe homecoming can help us remain calm. Stress affects everyone differently. The emergency response manager, who regularly practices for crisis may actually feel more alive during an event. The 78 year old diabetic grandmother who gets caught out in a storm without medication may panic so much she shuts down and isn't capable of doing even little things to help herself.

It is very important to remember how different we all are: we are the product of our experiences and upbringing, so no two people experience the same situation in the same way. For example, a woman who was sexually abused as a child told me that being in a dark cold car, surrounded by male strangers in their cars around her, triggered the trauma from her childhood at first. But once she connected with people on SnowedOutAtlanta, she realized that maybe the strangers in their cars around her might be "friends" so she bravely got out of her car and found a truck driver handing out food and drink to other women who were stranded and felt immediately so much better.

In a crisis, the more warning people have that a problem is coming, the better they are able to cope and prepare. If the crisis happens without warning, the fear response can cloud people's minds to such an extent that they are unable to help themselves, or are unable to remember more than a few facts. Here, Linda explains this phenomenon:

In advance of an event, officials give warnings that may trigger a memory—this is how we behaved last time; this is how to be safe this time. A warning must allow for information retrieval from memory so that it can be acted upon.

Risk Communication research has determined that people can only hold about seven pieces of data (information) in their mind at any one time. Dr. Victor Covello, a risk communications consultant, says under a situation of high stress government spokesman should say only 3 things[2]

Too many issues calling for attention may exceed the capacity of the person to act and they shut down in a stressful environment.

We also need to remember that even when warnings are given, different people react differently to those warnings, unless they are given very *specific* instructions of how to behave:

In risk communication, the experts look at both the hazard and the emotions expressed by the people about the risk. There is a scientific explanation – beyond just "fright or flight" reactions - for behavior in crisis situations. We know there is a small percentage of the public who will ignore storm warnings and will not seek shelter. When questioned these people usually have some variation of "last time it didn't get this bad" or "my family has always stayed in the house and we never had any problems before." It is clear that these people will not heed the government warnings to move. Then there are the shadow evacuees who will leave even when told that their location is safe. Further analysis of potential changes to official communications may help these outlier groups respond appropriately to evacuation messages.

---

[2] EPA guidelines for radiation emergency communications

I have talked to a lot of people who were on SnowedOutAtlanta during Snow Storm 1 - those looking for help for their loved ones, those in need of help themselves, as well as the "helpers." The range of emotions puzzled me at first, but having spoken to Linda, I have made some (partial) sense of it.

From Linda's analysis, I gather that the psychological responses I saw on SnowedOutAtlanta that night were very normal.

The extreme anxiety felt by people on the site who could not locate their loved ones, especially their children is something I had no trouble empathizing with at all. I know if I had been one of the parents missing a child on a school bus, I would not have been able to function enough to even use Facebook.

These women were very anxious but they felt comforted to find the SnowedOutAtlanta group because they at least knew that lots of people were looking out for their children. They felt supported and they also reported feeling the need to discuss the situation with others, to connect with others on the site (either by asking for prayers, or asking questions of others on the site or by asking for practical help) - all reactions that were completely normal.

I spoke to Linda about why a social media "group" helped so many people much more than simply receiving tweets via Twitter.  Linda says:

We know people cope better in groups, and that humans are capable of empathy and altruism – acts of compassion beyond our immediate family and friendship circle.  When we hear about someone in need of assistance, a pregnant woman stuck in a ditch, for example, there is a natural empathetic urge to help.   Individuals in trouble feel isolated, afraid and uncertain about which actions to take.

So it is a natural reaction to want to help others in a crisis, and one of the best ways to help individuals who are in trouble, is simply by connecting with them, supporting them.

Social media, in this case, the Facebook group for SnowedOutAtlanta, was a successful communication tool because it enabled people to reach out, and communicate with people nearby.  The media made friends of "strangers" - someone who might help.  By using your cell phone to access the internet you created the feeling of some sense of control (even if you were trapped in a car)  some connection to the larger community was created, knowing that there were people "out there" who were aware of your predicament and were trying to help you. This knowledge alone reduced stress levels and helped people calm down to help themselves.  Women trapped in their cars without winter clothes or boots were able to learn that the truck driver stuck next to their car actually had experience with bad weather and might have some food or water to share, instead of feeling like a potentially dangerous man was next to them.  Individuals with access to the internet were able to share nearby resources, whether that was an individual who offered a warm bed for the night, or a rescuer who could bring a blanket and warm cocoa to someone stuck on the highway.

The SnowedOutAtlanta Facebook group created an instant community of good Samaritans who could help by providing information and links from the warmth of their homes.  But it went further than that as the awareness of the site increased, people were able to use maps to narrow down the location of the people in most dire need of assistance and then locate other people close by, who volunteered to take water, food and blankets to those in need.  By tapping into our natural tendency to act altruistically, social media allows individuals to create informal assistance groups and take action.  There is a growing body of research that demonstrates that this altruistic behavior is genetic.

For those interested in the "in-depth" psychological reasons behind why people naturally want to help others, Linda provides research to back it up:

Prof. Paul Zak, an economist and neuroscientist at Claremont College in California wrote "The Moral Molecule"[3], about his extensive testing of human blood looking for oxytocin[4]. Oxytocin helps us form attachments such as the natural bonding of babies to their mothers and, along with serotonin and dopamine, flood the system with a sense of wellbeing. Oxytocin levels are related to how much we care for others (sympathy/empathy). His research shows how empathy and altruism created from the production of oxytocin enhance feelings of trust, cooperation, and love. He tests and measures the oxytocin levels with a trust game – a research tool in experimental economics.

### The Trust Game

Zak's Trust Game is conducted in a big room with 15-16 players the participant does not know. The participant sits in a cubicle with a computer. He reads the instructions on-line – just for showing up you receive $10 which is yours to keep. But you can receive more money by playing the game. The computer assigns a randomly chosen partner – Jane. If Jane will transfer part of her $10 to you, then you are given the opportunity to respond. According to the rules any amount she gives you, will triple in

---

[3] Moral Molecule, 2012

[4] a peptide that acts as both neurotransmitter, sending signals within the brain and a hormone that carries messages to the bloodstream

value when you receive it. Once you receive it you may, but you do not have to respond. The question is will you reciprocate? No social pressure - it is all anonymous. The more you play, the longer you exchange the more money you receive. Economists thought that with rational self-interest each person will decide based upon what is best for themselves, but Zak has discovered that people don't always make rational decisions, there are also emotions and other circumstances involved. He thinks that people behave depending upon how much oxytocin is released; based upon how trusted they felt when they reciprocated. He also found that when the original transfer was based on trust, there was a directly calibrated correspondence between the size of the transfer and the size of the recipient's response. The more money sent, the higher the oxytocin level he found in the blood, the more money was returned to player A. [5]

Prof. Zak has concluded that humans are wired to be trusting and skeptical, nurturing and punishing, competitive and cooperative, because each of these opposing forces can contribute to survival. He demonstrated how oxytocin was genetically selected over the millennia as a successful reproductive mechanism, as it helped our brains evolve to produce the opposite effect of flight or fight. William James, an experimental psychologist, defined emotions as the physiological changes your body undergoes when your senses pick up certain signals in the environment. [6] These emotional changes brought on by the release of oxytocin are almost instantaneous "without deliberate control and without conscious awareness[7]." When humans become aware of these sensations we label them feelings. Zak's research considered how being trusted encourages more generosity, even with strangers.

The flight or fight reaction - we call the emotion "fear" - is the brain's response to a real or imaginary threat. The amygdale is the part of the brain which triggers the response to flee by release of stress hormones - your heart thumps, your palms sweat etc. The emotional reaction, the "feeling," is labeled "afraid." Empathy, Zak says, is more subtle. He notes that animals bred without oxytocin have a kind of social amnesia, and he thinks that empathy requires a similar social memory at the cellular level. The sights and sounds of distress or trust or compassion trigger memories that allow us to access our earliest memories of our relationships to others, these memories trigger the release of the oxytocin. Humans have the ability to feel how another person is feeling. "Empathy, in effect, creates a physiological version of the golden rule." This means that when a situation we learn about causes us to do unto others as we would have them do unto us, it is in part because we are literally experiencing another person's pleasure/ pain as if it were our own. We can trace empathy from the initial surge in oxytocin, to the release of dopamine and serotonin that makes the experience both pleasurable and something you want to repeat, to the social engagement that emerges as a result.[8].

There are two types of stress – chronic and acute, Fear causes the hormone epinephrine to be released interfering with the oxytocin release – you get a charge of adrenaline instead. Normal stress, is caused by the release of cortisol. This increases your heart and blood rate to stimulate us into action, in the longer term it also creates high blood pressure, it liberates glucose etc. If the stress lasts – becomes chronic, then one can get heart disease and diabetes. These diseases also limit the release of oxytocin and they lower your empathy and compassion too. If your body produces too much cortisol this can lead to empathy fatigue – we get over exposed to bad news and shut down.

### The HOME circuit – Human Oxytocin Mediated Empathy Circuit [9]
Zak has described a circuit that is self re-enforcing, that allows us to behave morally. Most of the time, stress, testosterone, trauma, genetic anomalies and even mental conditioning can inhibit these effects but under normal conditions this HOME circuit works. Researchers know that high stress blocks oxytocin release, it not only drives empathetic concern/compassion, which might inhibit fighting for your life but it also damps down the amygdale, the brain structure that is where anxiety is registered and regulated. The tendency to judge rather than help is partly the result of a spot in the pre frontal cortex, full of oxytocin receptors, it appears to modulate the degree of empathy by regulating the release of dopamine in the HOME circuit. Oxytocin is the regulator between the self and other; between trust and distrust, between approach and withdrawal. When the oxytocin surge fades we move on from the feeling of empathy, the HOME circuit resets and we're ready to evaluate the next situation. When testosterone and other pro-punishment factors take over, we throw stones instead of a lifeline.

Therefore, what the SnowedOutAtlanta phenomena demonstrates is how powerful the empathy urge to action really is. When provided with a tool, in this case the ability to communicate across a region that was literally frozen in place, people's natural altruism led to hundreds of individuals taking whatever actions they were capable of, to help others.

---

[5] IBID p 15
[6] IBID p 56
[7] IBID p 57
[8] Ibid page 61
[9] Ibid page 62

Linda L Gunter began her career as a disaster volunteer after Hurricane Katrina in St. Bernard Parish, Louisiana, providing meals and first aid at a disaster relief center for six months. She spent six weeks in 2011 as a foreign media advisor to TEPCO after the Fukushima nuclear power station accident following the Japanese earthquake and tsunami. She has over 25 years' experience in various research/policy and communication roles related to nuclear energy. Gunter is currently researching a book on moral psychology and risk communications related to disaster relief.

# Chapter 5 – Disaster Management

Here in Atlanta, it's been painfully clear that government can't do it all, and just as clear that people can do a lot. That's a lesson worth remembering long after the last icicle melts.

(Tracy Hoover, Points of Light website)

I believe there are a lot of lessons that can be learned from both snow storms about disaster relief and disaster management.

As the quote above says, the primary lesson we need to learn is that people can do a lot to help themselves. We also need to learn that there are some emergencies that make it very difficult for the emergency services to get to the people who need help and therefore, the emergency management structure needs to cater to and plan for situations where people *have to* help themselves.

Although in this situation, many mistakes were made, and many things that should have been done were not done properly, we should not forget that even in cases where everything is done correctly, there may be times when the emergency services cannot get to the people in need of help.

For those cases where doing things "properly" can help avoid catastrophe, we should ensure that those things are done properly in future. For example, in Georgia, residents have known for a long time that the State is very ill-equipped to deal with snowstorms. It has been a long-standing joke about the number of snow plows and how little sanding equipment Georgia has. Assuming that the State is not going to suddenly make a huge investment in snow-handling equipment to cater for incidents that happen very rarely, given our geography, it is therefore extremely important that the State government be overly cautious whenever snow is likely to appear, especially when it is likely to appear during a school day or a work day. Schools must be closed and people must be told not to go out unless it is an emergency. Companies should be told to close down for the day in such situations.

For those cases where emergency services simply cannot get to those in need, the national incident management system (NIMS) and the agencies involved in emergency management - from FEMA down to the EMAs, from government departments to companies, from official disaster management agencies and groups to NGOs (non-governmental organizations) like the Red Cross) - need to have procedures in place that take into account the fact that people can help themselves in circumstances when the current official structure just does not work.

We have to prepare and empower people so that they can help themselves in such emergencies. I suggest that we can do this partly via social media, but also through encouraging training and information sharing within our communities, for example, through the FEMA website (http://training.fema.gov has some great online training anyone can do at any time) , CERT training and other initiatives.

## Disaster Management – Before

Humans are fallible. GEMA and the governor's office clearly made big mistakes before and during Snow Storm 1.

By 11 a.m., heavy snow was falling in some areas

At 12:15 p.m., schools were letting out

At 1 p.m., Atlanta city government closes

By 2 p.m., Gridlock

At 5 p.m., GEMA finally goes online.

Charley English, who is not only head of GEMA but is also president of the National Emergency Management Association and has a Masters degree in Homeland Defense and Security, admitted he got it wrong:

"I got this one wrong.. I got it wrong by six hours."

If he got it wrong, anyone can.

Governor Deal said:

"I think we did not respond fast enough.. We did not respond in the magnitude and at an early enough time to be able to avoid some of these consequences."

Many blame GEMA, citing an email from Deal's chief of staff to Charley English of GEMA:

"Everyone keeps trying to tell me how bad the weather is going to be but I keep saying if the weather was going to be bad, Charlie would have called and he hasn't called me."[10]

I think the "blame game" deflects attention from the *real problem*: It does not really matter who got it wrong because our emergency management procedures should work even when someone gets it wrong. We should have had a "Plan B" in place for this kind of scenario. For example, a large-scale chemical attack by terrorists might similarly cause chaos on our roads and incapacitate a lot of people driving at the time of the attack enough so that our roads were inaccessible in many areas. Our emergency management system needs to work in such situations.

[10] 11Alive News website articles were used to construct this section, primarily this one: http://www.11alive.com/news/article/320309/40/Emails-reveal-failure-with-GEMA-director-on-snow-mobilization

Primarily, a new approach to information management and information sharing is needed. In the case of Snow Storm 1, my SnowedOutAtlanta group would have been empty if GEMA already had a social group on its website sharing information about the current situation, allowing people to swap tips about which roads were closed and which alternative routes were available. The group wouldn't have been necessary if there had been available information about a plethora of official Red Cross shelters available to anyone stranded, or if people had known that a "State of Emergency" meant that they could show up at any open supermarket or any one of many stores (Home Depots for example) and could get warmth, food and water. The problem is that GEMA did not have this information on its site, and it was unclear what a "State of Emergency" meant for the ordinary person.

GEMA needs to have a site like that. Let's call it the "HelpGeorgia" website. Somewhere that everyone in Georgia knows to go to find out this kind of information in an emergency. People should not have to go separately to the Red Cross site and try to work out how to use the Shelter Finder app to find out where the nearest shelter is. The shelter finder should be integrated within the "HelpGeorgia" site.

People should not have to hunt around the web for local police phone numbers because they cannot get through to 911. Firstly, all the local police phone numbers and local police websites should be available on the "HelpGeorgia" website. Secondly, someone should *always* answer a 911 call. This "HelpGeorgia" site should also include guidance to people looking for different types of help. For example, something like this might have been appropriate in Snow Storm 1:

1. If you have a life threatening emergency, call 911 (goes through to secondary tier if overwhelmed, so hold the line please)
2. If you have a minor injury, go to one of these locations: [link to list of locations available]
3. If you have had a car accident but no one is injured, call 511 or call AAA on this number XXX XXX XXXX. If no one answers leave a voicemail and they will tow your car away when resources allow. Leave your car in place if you are unable to move it off of the road but leave your keys in the car glove compartment.
4. If you are a pregnant woman or have a baby or children in the car, call the National Guard on this number XXX XXX XXXX
5. If you are able to get to a shelter here is a list of official shelters [link to list of shelters]
6. Shops and locations available as makeshift shelters are listed here [link to companies/churches operating as makeshift shelters]

All social media feeds should feed into one large database that is searchable using a powerful search engine within this "HelpGeorgia" website. The user should be able to select feeds based on type (weather reports, shelter locations, police phone numbers, etc.) and based on location (e.g. county, city or postal code). It is very important that location search is flexible, as many people affected by a disaster are from out of town and do not know which county or zipcode they are in. A number of people driving through the Atlanta area were helped on the SnowedOutAtlanta group because they did not know this kind of location information and because of that were unable to find local help.

I also think another lesson that should be learned is that there are many communities who feel excluded from the disaster management/relief process. I explore the issues surrounding one community, the disabled community, in depth below. However, another community I was very acutely aware of during the storms was the Hispanic-speaking community (Spanish or Portuguese speaking). There appeared to be few resources to send them to help them and I was ashamed that I could not find any.

I wish I was qualified to help them but I speak so little Spanish! I hope someone will champion their cause.

I believe that the whole premise behind disaster relief/disaster management (NIMS structure) needs to change. The basic premise behind the current structure is that ordinary people cannot help themselves until someone "official" gets on the scene, i.e. someone who has been trained in at least the basics of how to manage incidents – an "Incident Commander."

I believe that the NIMS structure needs to be modified, probably simply added to, to accommodate those scenarios where no "Incident Commander" can actually get to the scene of an incident. It needs to be modified to take into account situations where the only people on the ground do not have formal NIMS training, situations where no emergency personnel of any kind are able to get to those in need of help. It needs to take into account the huge extent to which those people can help themselves and others, without the help of the emergency services.

Of course, there are limitations on how much "ordinary people" can help themselves and others, but I believe Snow Storm 1 proved that those limitations are not as great as some in the NIMS structure would have us believe. But it also showed that the current NIMS structure does not handle some situations and that there *are* situations where emergency services personnel, and real "Incident Commanders" cannot make it to the scene of incidents. We must again remember that this is the case not only during snow storms but also during hurricanes and floods (of course the prime example of this is during Katrina), earthquakes and tsunamis (the U.S. could feasibly face a disaster similar to the one we saw in Fukushima, Japan).

In such disasters, psychological studies have shown that the survival rate increases dramatically if the people affected at least have a plan of action, if they at least know something they can do to help themselves or others, and also if they feel connected to others who want to help them (whether via emotional support or practical help or just by providing information).

When accessible, social media can be a large part of that emotional/psychological support, as well as the information provision, and in some cases it can also provide practical help (for example, on SnowedOutAtlanta, where people offered their own homes as shelters to anyone stuck in the snow).

I believe another huge part of preparing individuals is through education and training. I fully support the CERT (Community Emergency Response Training) program. I am personally "CERT-trained" and, as a result, I know the basics of first aid, light search and rescue and a little about how the authorities deal with crises. I know a great deal about how my local EMA (Cobb Emergency Management Association), GEMA (Georgia Emergency Management Association) and FEMA (Federal Emergency Management Association) work together in a crisis also because I took a few FEMA courses – courses that anyone can take in their own time via the FEMA website – http://training.fema.gov . I strongly encourage everyone to do so.

I, of course, had a number of questions about the current way emergency management appears to work in Georgia.

For example, I wondered why the Red Cross did not open many shelters during Snow Storm 1. In fact, I am aware of only one shelter they opened – in Sandy Springs (Hammond Drive). I learned that under NIMS, the Red Cross cannot open a shelter without being asked to do so by GEMA (or in some cases the governor's office). Even when they are asked to open a shelter, their shelters are supposedly "long term shelters" only, so in this case shelters were deemed inappropriate.

I, like many others, find it very strange that the Red Cross had volunteers willing to open shelters, and they had food, drink and blankets that could have been of use to those who were stranded, and yet the shelters were not "activated." One Red Cross source quoted "transportation problems" saying that shelter equipment could not be driven to "appropriate locations." It is my view that wherever that equipment was located was an "appropriate location" that night, as people were stranded across the metro Atlanta area. If an official shelter could not have been opened, at the very least, the volunteers could have taken blankets, food and drink out to people's cars. Or, if they felt it was too dangerous, they could have let the public know where to come and get the supplies from, and the general public could have picked up the supplies.

I believe that the main Red Cross shelters should immediately be opened in a scenario like Snow Storm 1; GEMA should not wait for a "long-term emergency" to activate Red Cross shelters – they need to find a way to open shelters in situations like Snow Storm 1.

Another question I have is why more CERT personnel were not "activated." Again, CERT personnel are not *allowed* to operate until they have been "activated" – which involves being "checked in" by an "Incident Commander." In this instance, in some areas, no attempt was made to activate them to my knowledge, although I know that some were activated in Douglas County. Community Emergency Response Teams are trained in basic first aid, light search and rescue and general emergency management principles. These personnel could have handed out blankets, food and water to those in their cars also, and perhaps could have helped with first aid of some of the less serious injuries. I know Leticia Mathis of Douglas County and Bernard King of Cobb County are actively involved in ramping up CERT volunteers and training as part of her "lessons learned" from Snow Storm 1. I hope that is also the case in other counties and I hope if a similar situation arises in the future, more CERT volunteers would be activated.

I also have questions about the schools and school buses. There seemed to be some "rules" that could not be broken during Snow Storm 1 even in cases where sticking to the rules could seriously affect the health of a child. I understand the need to have rules that children should not be let off of a school bus in normal situations, but in this situation, I think the rules should have been bent to allow children to use rest rooms or to get warm (with close supervision from the school bus drivers, of course), and I believe most parents agree with me. I understand the need for rules preventing anyone from giving food to children on school buses under normal circumstances, but in this case I think some exceptions should have been made.

Another concern I have, and this one is probably the most serious, is that 911 was completely overwhelmed during Snow Storm 1. People got "busy" signals when they called 911, or they held the line and it rang and rang, with no answer.  This was extremely scary for those in need of help and added to the psychological issues created by the snow storm itself.

I understand that funding of Public Safety is a big issue in Cobb County (according to Jack Forsythe, see a snippet from his letter below) and I understand in other parts of Georgia also, and that is one of the reasons Cobb County 911 calls were not answered as they should have been.   I do not know if this was the case in other parts of the Atlanta metro area or not.

However, it is very evident from the results of my investigation and analysis, that Public Safety in Cobb County has suffered from a lack of sufficient funding and resources to properly sustain the appropriate level of personnel, facilities, and equipment needed to provide an adequate level of protection for the citizens of Cobb County. This lack of support for public safety over the years has increased officer safety issues, reduced the number of officers available for calls, increased fire response times and ultimately the degradation of the morale of all public safety personnel.  As a result of these outstanding issues there is an immediate need for a major infusion of resources to enhance the public safety resources in Cobb County. This critical need has now been exacerbated

Of course, the ideal solution would be to increase funding to Public Safety, and I am certainly of the opinion that this is an extremely important issue (especially in Cobb County, which is the county I live in, where other local issues will make this even more important in years to come, as the Braves Stadium comes to Cobb County).

However, even without that extra funding, procedures can be put into place in cases of emergency whereby if people cannot get through to 911, they should get redirected to a secondary "tier" of help – maybe 911 in other parts of the country (who could at least advise people over the phone of their best course of action), or 511 in the case of the Atlanta Snow Storm 1 – or maybe Georgia Power in the case of Snow Storm 2.  I have also heard suggestions that specially trained secondary "tier" personnel could be used to man 911 in extreme emergencies (CERT personnel for example) and I believe that is a great option also.

A secondary "tier" is a great idea because, contrary to popular belief, most calls received by 911 in situations like this really are *not* emergencies!  I have listened to those in local EMA's and 911 operators talk about how many calls they received from people asking questions that could easily have been answered by going to the SnowedOutAtlanta group – questions like "Where is my nearest gas station?" or "Can someone pick up my kids from school?"  The secondary "tier" personnel could deal with most of the calls without the expertise of 911 operators but should have a direct line through to the Emergency Operations Center for cases where a real emergency *has* bubbled down to them.

Also, in a "State of Emergency" it is my understanding that the National Guard should supplement the emergency services and 911 teams.  In the case of Snow Storm 1, many of us tried to call the official National Guard phone number provided by GEMA for cases we felt were extreme emergencies (where babies or children's lives were at risk for example).  However, the National Guard phone number was apparently so overloaded that the number was redirected to Sandy Springs police personnel who were unable to help, however dire the situation.  This cannot be allowed to happen.  When people really need help they need to be able to get through to 911 or the National Guard.

I also have concerns with the way in which lessons learned from Snow Storm 1 are being processed.

Governor Deal, to his credit, has been very proactive about rectifying the issues that caused Snow Storm 1 to be such a traumatic experience for so many.  His plan includes a "Severe Weather Task Force" which will look into:

- how the state and communities within the state can be better prepared in the future

- how weather predictions can be better used in the future

- how long-term preparations can be made better in the future for emergencies

- how severe weather warnings can be implemented better

- communications improvements related to severe weather

- actions once (severe) weather occurs

- actions after (severe) weather occurs

- standing down after such events

I am extremely glad that Governor Deal has taken this issue very seriously and is moving forward with finding solutions to the problems highlighted by the snow storm.

My concerns with Governor Deal's plan include the fact that it concerned only severe weather events, and did not handle the countless other disaster scenarios that citizens now fear Georgia is ill-prepared for.  I believe his Task Force *will* come up with a better way to handle future snow storms, but I am not confident that they will be able to handle very well a different scenario that results in many cars strewn across multiple highways and roads with many people in need of help inaccessible to emergency crews very well.  Such a scenario might result from, for example, a mass terrorist (e.g. chemical) attack.  Although such scenarios are improbable, we should learn as many lessons as we can from this situation to help us if such a scenario arose.

I also think it is very important that future plans take into account the role of social media in disaster management/relief.  I was not asked to give input to the governor's Severe Weather Task Force.

If I had been, the main message I would have provided would be that the disaster management/relief efforts need to support the individual/family in helping themselves or those close to them.

One way people can do this in a crisis is via social media.  Currently, there are hundreds of sources of disaster management-related social media in Georgia alone (see http://emergency20wiki.org/wiki/index.php/Georgia_emergency_agencies_using_social_media), but in a crisis, the individual does not have time to search each of these sources for the information they need.

What is needed is one central source of all information.

As I suggest above, I recommend a "HelpGeorgia" website within which individuals can search for the information they need. I suggest "HelpGeorgia" should be built as an extension to WebEOC (the system connecting many of the parties involved in emergency management) and could include a disaster relief database which contains all tweets and Facebook posts from all these sources along with a website with a great search engine that allows the individual to search for the information that they need.

WebEOC already has the technical infrastructure needed to tie most of the agencies involved together, and presumably is already resilient, robust and reliable in the manner you would expect of a disaster management system:

Today, WebEOC is not only used by government agencies such as the U.S. Departments of Agriculture, Defense, Energy, Homeland Security (CDP, FEMA, ICE, TSA, and USCG), Health and Human Services, EPA, and NASA, but also by corporations, public utilities, universities, and more.

(GEMA website)

My last concern is that the community needs to be better educated. One big concern is that no one appears to know what the term "State of Emergency" means in Georgia in terms that the ordinary person can understand. People need to know what it means for them. Does it mean that they can call the National Guard? If so, in which situations may they be called? Does it mean that they should not go to work? Does it mean that if they run a supermarket they should keep it open? I would like the authorities to put out a definitive list of what a "State of Emergency" means, in terms of what being in that state means for businesses, individuals and for the National Guard and the emergency services.

Also, community members need to know how to get different kinds of help so that 911 is not overloaded with calls and requests. Douglas County, again, has "Community Education" in this area on its list of "Lessons Learned" and "Improvements." I hope that all parties involved (at the county level, city level and state levels) also learn this lesson.

My initial proposal on the future of disaster management was posted on SnowedOutAtlanta at the end of January 2014:

**Michelle Sollicito**

Proposals/improvements suggested by me so far as a result of the work we have done since last Tuesday:

Governor Deal:
1. As it seems unlikely we should provide realistic snow handling equipment in this State given the rarity of such events, we recommend being OVERLY cautious in relation to snow events. If snow of more than one inch is predicted by The Weather Channel top meteorologists in an area during the working day, we suggest ALL SCHOOLS in that area should be closed for the day, and a recommendation that people do not drive unless it is an emergency should be issued. This will at least reduce the number of people on the roads, and reduce the number of children on the roads.

GEMA:
1. Collaborate with Google Maps team ▮▮▮▮▮▮▮ on how to use Google Maps for Emergencies. Do this in conjunction with Jelena Crawford, Rachel Bruce and Michelle Sollicito from SnowedOutAtlanta as we know the benefits and shortcomings of Google Maps and we know how to overcome them also. E.g. Security and Privacy issues can easily be overcome using the Google Maps API with a few days coding. E.g we need to build in LAYERS - one layer of permanent map residents (hospitals, police stations, fire stations are always there), another layer for semi-permanent residents (e.g locations that will always be open in any State of Emergency) and a layer for "current emergency only" (e.g. Joe Doe offers his home to anyone caught in the snow tonight. He is in the Powers Ferry Rd / Delk Rd area. If you would like to stay, call this number XXX-XXXX-XXXX)

2. We need a CENTRAL Database with an EXCELLENT search engine, with high reliability and robustness/failover/redundancy built in. This central database should capture all the resources, tweets and facebook posts of all the various agencies offering help in a crisis. The average Joe does not have time to search the websites, tweets and facebook posts of all these agencies (See http://emergency20wiki.org/wiki/index.php /Georgia_emergency_agencies_using_social_media). The search engine should also take feeds from the Red Cross Shelter Finder App and other non-governmental agencies that help in a crisis.

DOT:

1. During emergency evacuations, have only one lane open going INTO the city, and all other lanes going OUT of the city on all major highways.

2. If 511 is overloaded (take all precautions so that it is NOT overloaded), have it redirect calls to AAA and allow them to call out local towing companies for no cost to the stranded / person in accident

3. ALL DOT vehicles should have chains in their trunks in case of snow. ALL Emergency vehicles AND SCHOOL BUSES should also carry chains in case of snow.

Average Joe:

1. Create an Emergency Preparedness kit in any location you might need it (e.g. one for work, one for home, one in the car). For now, this is a good link for this but we are coming up with a succinct list and will publish soon http://www.redcross.org/prepare/location/home-family/get-kit

2. Buy a Weather Radio at the very least (and make sure you know how to use it). If you want to go further, you can buy CB Radio or even HAM Radio equipment. We will provide a document advising you on this in the near future.

Facebook:

1. A list of improvements has been sent to Facebook indicating the issues we had on Snow Tuesday night using Facebook. Although Facebook was an awesome tool and worked very well in many respects (e.g. by "liking" a post or comment, people could ensure those most in need of help got pushed to the top of the page and therefore got more help from people who could help them, also the sheer numbers meant there were lots of options open to those stranded in the snow - we could offer advice on which roads were impassible, which gas stations were open nearby, where the nearest Home Depot or Walgreens or Kroger was offering shelter and food, etc.) there were some issues and limitations with Facebook. The Facebook team is working on improving all those issues with me right now.

SnowedOutAtlanta

1. SnowedOutAtlanta was created on the fly to deal with an unexpected situation. In future emergencies we will have a more organized approach. We are coming up with a new structure to include new groups and sub groups and we will have a tagging system to enable people to search for posts and comments that are most useful to them. If Facebook does not fix their tagging I will write a search engine myself to overcome this issue as it is fairly easy to do.

The most important recommendation I have is that social media can empower ordinary people to help themselves and each other in a crisis.

One way communication via social media (e.g. Twitter tweets or Facebook page posts) can help a great deal, but I recommend Facebook **groups** to enable people to support one another, connect with one another and share information with one another as I believe such a mechanism is more effective in some scenarios.

In other recent disasters, the power of one way social media (in this case, Twitter tweets) has been seen in communicating with people:

Emily Rahimi, the New York City Fire Department's social media manager, used Twitter to help calm people and dispense information during Hurricane Sandy. Here is a clip from an interview with her:

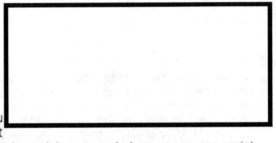

**How have things changed as far as social media use since those two days during Sandy?**
The hurricane really got people to understand a little bit more, at least around here, how social media can be very important in terms of communications. They had been hesitant about it because if you're not familiar with social media, you might focus on what could go wrong with it or how it can be used improperly. But I think that really opened people's eyes as to how we can use social media as a great tool to communicate with the public, let them know what's going on within the department as well as how to prepare for emergencies. That's been helpful because it's enabled me to get a lot more cooperation and maybe open more doors in terms of finding ways to use social media to help more groups in the department. It's growing and great to see.

(govtech.com)

As many as 52,000 people were able to access the FDNY's "tweets" and get information that was being dispensed, which was wonderful and probably saved many lives. It was especially useful in a crisis where few people had power and many people could only access information using their cellphones.

However, because it was one-way communication, Emily was the only one dispensing information. She had to work extremely hard to keep answering every tweet that came in from the public. This was a one-way broadcast scenario, great for getting information from one central source out to many people, but not great at leveraging the knowledge and help of many people to directly help others.

In scenarios where a Facebook group is accessible (i.e. where there is no power outage, or where those in need can make cellphone calls for help to people who have power), it is much more efficient and effective way to share information in a crisis and for the public to support and help one another, rather than rely on a single source of information.

The power of those in need of help being able to share information, get advice, interact with others who are familiar with the area cannot be over-emphasized. The Facebook group helped people psychologically and emotionally.

## New Technologies for Disaster Management

There are many new technologies that can improve disaster management – especially those which empower individuals to help themselves and their families.

I know that GTRI (Georgia Tech Research Institute) is doing a lot of investigations into the potential use of drones. They are probably already investigating the use of drones in disaster relief scenarios, but if they are not I highly recommend they do so. Although the technology is fraught with difficulties and is very expensive to produce, the use of drones to deliver medicines, food, drink to those in need would be invaluable. They could also deliver diapers and formula to mothers stranded with babies, life jackets to those who are in danger of drowning, blankets to those in danger of hypothermia, tools (hammers, saws etc.) to those who are trapped, etc. Drones may also be a more efficient way of distributing salt to the roads in cases where the roads are so icy that the snowplows cannot get through.

For more information on this exciting technological concept, see this great TED talk by Andreas Raptopoulos:

http://www.ted.com/talks/andreas_raptopoulos_no_roads_there_s_a_drone_for_that

There are also many smartphone apps being developed which have exciting potential in the disaster management area. I have evaluated a number of these since Snow Storm 1 but feel unable to recommend most of them until I have seen them "in action" or I have had more input from others who have used them "in action" but I highly recommend that we all try downloading some of them just in case we need them.

In particular, Georgia Power has a number of apps that can be used on most smartphones that were very useful during Snow Storm 2, and the Weather Channel has an outstanding app for the desktop:

# Download Desktop Weather App for Windows

### Windows 7, Windows Vista and Windows XP

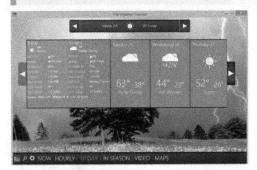

You get the most accurate desktop weather experience by combining our patented forecasting technology and the expertise of our 200 meteorologists. No other desktop app compares for providing severe weather alerts, forecasts, radar, as well as premium video content directly to your desktop produced by the industry leader, The Weather Channel.

### Windows 8.0 and Windows 8.1

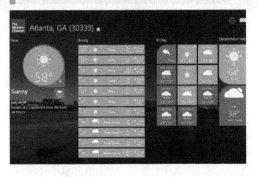

The Windows 8 upgrade now includes our ultra-local TruPoint™ forecasting technology to provide you with the most accurate weather forecast available. Get current weather as live tiles and rich-imagery on your desktop update to reflect outdoor conditions at-a-glance and provide a direct link into our app when you want more weather details.

## It also has an app for all other platforms:

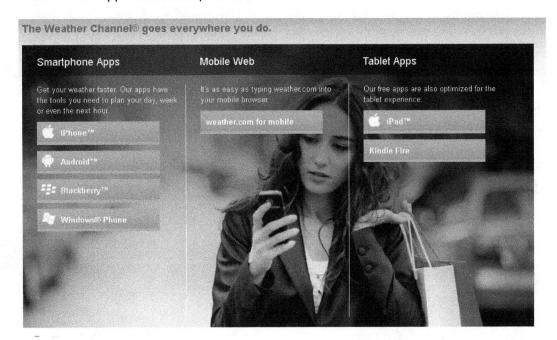

# Including People with Disabilities During a Crisis

During Snow Storm 1, I became acutely aware that there were a number of communities who were "left out in the cold." One community I was extremely concerned about, but felt inadequate to help with, was the disabled community.

They had trouble accessing information that would help them during the snow storm. I know how difficult it is to make a website "accessible" because my husband, who has worked for Yahoo! for many years, was once tasked with making some of Yahoo!'s websites accessible, and I know how much work was involved in making them so.

I know a lot of people who make websites are completely unaware of how difficult it is for Disabled people to access them, although there are now a great number of tools and tags at the disposal of website developers to help the blind, deaf and other disabled people to use websites. Because "accessibility" of Facebook was causing the disabled community so many problems I did all I could to try to help them, but I felt it wasn't enough.

Luckily, halfway through the first night of snow storm 1, I found the following page which helped a great many of the disabled members of SnowedOutAtlanta:

https://www.facebook.com/help/accessibility

Also, I met online a wonderful lady named Laura George, who is a full-time, professional advocate for disabled people, and has a particular interest in their interests during crises because she experienced a hurricane with her disabled husband. Her husband has since died, sadly, but Laura has put all her energies since that time into helping others in similar predicaments.

As a result of her experiences with SnowedOutAtlanta and other emergencies, Laura has come up with some guidance for those with disabilities in preparing for disasters. Many of these are useful for able-bodied people to bear in mind also. Here are her top 10 notes in this area (actually she ended up with 11!):

1. Have at least one weeks' worth of back-up supplies (both hardware and software).
2. Have at least one weeks' worth of extra medication (some insurance companies will make provision for this.) If refrigeration is required look into portable refrigeration packs that do not require electricity.
3. If you rely upon another person to help you conduct your daily living activities, find two more people (at least) who can serve as back-up if they can't help in an emergency.
4. Life Sustaining Medical Equipment: have portable back-up power options readily available. If your ability to survive is threatened with loss of electricity (breathing, sweating, medical equipment) contact your utility companies (with a doctor's note) and make them aware of your situation.
5. Technology that allows for communication, mobility, hearing aids, etc., in life.. make sure that you have portable back-up options. If you can carry these with you all the better. Also take along model & serial numbers in case you need to have your equipment replaced.
6. Get medic alert jewelry. This will speak for you when no one else is around to speak for you and you can't speak for yourself.
7. Have a community plan: Back up caregivers, neighbors who know your situation, family and loved ones, out-of-town contacts (especially usefully in Hurricane Andrew!).
8. Pack a manual can-opener not an electric one.

9. Have 6 plans for sheltering. Three for *inside* your home: #1 you hope for, #2, when #1 fails, and #3 for the evacuation if your home gets damaged. Three for sheltering *outside* the home: #1 you hope for, #2 when that fails, and #3 because it's good to have!
10. Caregivers: Speak with your local fire department, health department and in-home medical services to see what education they have and/or that you can share with them to create a plan for the one you care about.
11. Remember - it is your responsibility to be emergency aware at all times and have a plan.

## General points that Laura recommends disabled people should bear in mind include:

1. Until someone comes to your aid, you are the first responder on the scene. Then it gets handed off to the person who is helping you.
2. No one knows the challenges you face unless you speak up for yourself!
3. If you need assistance in designing your plan it is your responsibility to ask for assistance from the community.
4. If you ask the community for help, then it is the community's responsibility to help create resources and plans that will help you have a complete plan to rely upon in a disaster.
5. If you can't find a solution to the challenge you face in creating your plan, or have trouble getting assistance to address a concern with it: reach out to your local State ADA Coordinator's Office.
6. Get involved and find out what your community is doing with emergency planning.

### Random Thoughts/ Lessons Learned

1. From now on, when a warning is issued I will not let my child go to school. If I have 12 hours' notice, then I will plan for no school the following day. I can always take them in late.
2. Create more electrical power back up for the technology I use. (As I was running a county emergency preparedness Facebook site actively, it occurred to me I didn't have a solid plan to keep the site going for power loss. So I forewarned of movement to my personal Twitter account.)
3. Media needed to be more sensitive to the needs of the Deaf and Hard of Hearing communities. Tickers across the screen told of school closings but not what was being said of the news in terms of governmental direction through the storm. ASL interpreters for those in persons in Deaf and Hard of Hearing Communities were all but non-existent. So if your first language is ASL you only learned what you could about the storm through your own personal network.
4. Dialysis and cardiac consumers dependent on breathing machines and treatments clearly have not been given education on how to prepare themselves for weather emergent events.
5. Too many stories of pregnant moms being caught without shelter or assistance in the storm. Again, there should have been proactive education given!
6. Emergency Management Agencies and similar organizations in a disaster would do well to enact social media resources to help reduce calls on the phone and to supplement for the lack of information given in a local community that might be seeing extreme events.
7. Short frustration list:
    1. Lack of identifiable sheltering
    2. Lack of communication with the deaf
    3. Very apparent lack of pre-education to those with functional needs
    4. Total disregard for "warning" observance by communities and schools of dangerous weather
    5. Why is french toast (ie. bread & milk) so popular to make in a disaster?
8. Appreciate the kind notes of follow-up and thanks for pre-awareness by many of my friends in the paralysis community.
9. Too much finger pointing at whose fault it was. Not enough inclusion of the community to help collaborate on the solutions. Weather can't address medical needs.
10. "To fight for your beliefs, you must believe in your fights. To succeed you must get others to believe too." Yes that's my quote. Now you know why I educate and advocate in emergency management and the disability communities as well as others.

For those interested in helping disabled people in crises, please contact Laura George using email address educateandadvocate@gmail.com. Here is her amazing bio:

Laura George is an Emergency Management Disability Liaison who directly works with the first responding and disability communities encouraging collaboration and better emergency disaster planning between them. Her work in this field was prompted by the simultaneous paralysis of her spouse while being pregnant and addressing a hurricane. She is a program director, presenter, educator, advocate, and published writer sitting on committees from the local to national levels. She has a Bachelor's of Science degree; certificates from the Emergency Management Institute; a Basic Disaster Life Support and Community Emergency Response Team, along with many others. Ms. George has received many awards and accolades for her uncharted work. She is on many committees including the National Center for Independent Living - Emergency Preparedness committee, the Georgia Emergency Preparedness Coalition for Individuals with Disabilities and Older Adults at the Georgia State ADA Offices, the Gwinnett Coalition for Health & Human Services - Emergency Preparedness Coalition and many others.

In addition, FEMA has a course aimed at helping us include those with disabilities during a crisis.

http://training.fema.gov/EMIWeb/IS/courseOverview.aspx?code=IS-368

## Thank You Facebook!

I realize that without Facebook, SnowedOutAtlanta could not have happened.  So I want to end this book by including a message I sent to Mark Zuckerberg thanking him for his wonderful creation.

Mark

I just want to thank you for being such an inspiration to me, and I am sure so many others!

Facebook enabled me to help thousands of people in one night (via my group SnowedOutAtlanta) and I doubt there is another tool that would have stood up to 50,000 people all joining a group within 24 hours, and posting at a rate of 100 posts per minute for HOURS, both via pc browsers and via smartphones and devices.  Incredible!

I hope you are extremely proud of what you have achieved!

I know you are the kind of guy for whom money is not the motivator, but helping people IS.  So you should feel extremely satisfied that you have achieved what you set out to do (and I am sure there is a lot more to come!)

You have made people in the world feel more connected, you have made them more altruistic and you have empowered them to help more people.

Gandhi would be proud of you for embodying his phrase that I know you quote often: "Be the change you want to see in the world"

You are change!

We are Atlanta!

Michelle Sollicito

SnowedOutAtlanta

# Appendix 1 Notes

[BOX] Note that in the main text above, wherever you see boxes like this, they are hiding personal information or information the poster no longer wants to be public such as phone numbers or urls.

# Appendix 2 The Pinned Post

Here I am listing a snapshot of the pinned post we used during Snow Storm 1, as many people have asked what kind of information to include in such a post during a disaster. Of course, this pinned post was constantly updated, so this is just one snapshot of many versions of that pinned post. Note that, of course, many of these links and phone numbers may now be out of date but the post is useful as a reference.

PLEASE READ THIS FIRST!!

(this page will be constantly updated also - if you have something to add PM me)

If you have a life-threatening emergency first call 911. After that consider the resources below.

SHELTERS

=======

To find a shelter, or to provide a shelter please see this link. There is a link to a form you fill in to add an address as a shelter and there is the link to the map so you can see all current shelters also.

https://www.facebook.com/photo.php?fbid=10151908613968247&set=gm.408395582639791&type=1&theater

Emergency RSS Feeds

==============

I am testing out a new web tool that hopefully contains all the Emergency feeds you are likely to need over the coming few days - right now there is nothing much on it of course, but it will show its worth over the next few days I hope. I have not had time to create the full system I want to create so this is a "First step" so please bear that in mind when using it!

http://output29.rssinclude.com/output?type=fb&id=835708&hash=0b8f685707dd08ead13166fc73a500e4

NOTE GEMA FEEDS show as ERRORS but if you click on them, then in the new window, remove the ? (question mark) and anything AFTER it, and then press press ENTER (Return) it should work

GEMA now has a similar tool that is quite good see

http://m.fema.gov/social-hub

You can see most of these here too

https://www.facebook.com/pages/Atlantaemergencyfeeds/297681503714489

The idea behind this is to prevent everyone having to go to 100 different websites to get the latest info.

Contact/Useful info

=====================

Warming Centers,Shelters etc

http://www.gema.ga.gov/content/forms/ShelterInformation.pdf

Useful info, up to date

http://www.wsbradio.com/news/news/atlanta-traffic/nC7qX/

Police Precincts open for stranded motorists

http://www.gema.ga.gov/content/forms/PolicePrecinctsOpenForStrandedMotorists.pdf

School Closing info http://www.wsbtv.com/school-closings/search/

511 - Current Road situation map with cameras

http://www.511ga.org/

GEMA

Website: http://www.gema.ga.gov

E-mail:pao@gema.ga.gov

Phone: (404) 635-7000 or1-(800)-TRY-GEMA (1-800-879 4362)

Red Cross

http://www.redcross.org

Marietta

Call 770-794-5334 and the Marietta Police Department will assist you.

Kennesaw

Call 770-422-2505 and the Kennesaw Police Department will assist you.

Atlanta Police Dept

(404) 614-6544

https://www.facebook.com/AtlantaPoliceDpt

www.Twitter.com/atlanta_police

Cobb County Govt

http://portal.cobbcountyga.gov/index.php

Cobb County Police

770) 499-3900

Cobb DOT

(770) 528-1600

http://portal.cobbcountyga.gov/index.php?option=com_content&id=599&Itemid=299

Get Ready

http://ready.ga.gov

Red Cross shelter finder

http://app.redcross.org/nss-app/

USGS

http://earthquake.usgs.gov

National Weather Service

https://www.weather.gov


City of Atlanta

http://www.atlantaga.gov

on Facebook

www.facebook.com/cityofatlanta


Atlanta Fire Rescue Dept

www.facebook.com/atlantafirerescue


Atlanta Airport

www.facebook.com/hartsfieldjackson

http://atlanta-airport.com/


Mayor Kasim Reed www.Twitter.com/kasimreed


POWER OUTAGES

===========

GENERATORS - if you are using one, please read this!!

http://www.nsc.org/news_resources/Resources/Documents/Portable_Generator_Safety_Tips.pdf


Georgia Power - Ice Storm Tips (Also report an outage here)

================================

http://georgiapower.com/in-your-community/storm-center/before/prepare-icestorm.cshtml


Useful info when preparing for outages

=========================

http://www.myajc.com/news/news/the-dark-side-avoiding-power-outage-problems/ndKJJ/?icmp=ajc_internallink_invitationbox_apr2013_ajcstubtomyajcpremium

Report outages at Marietta Power and Water

=============================

To report a non-emergency problem: call 770-794-5160

Power-related emergencies: 770-794-5160

Other Utilities in the Marietta area

=====================

Marietta City Utilities Board

675 N Marietta Pky Ne

Marietta

(770) 794-5192

Cobb Electric Membership Cor...

1000 Emc Pky Ne

Marietta

(770) 429-2100

Marietta City Water Department

627 N Marietta Pky Ne, ?#?B?

Marietta

(770) 794-5230

Industrial Power & Components ...

1536 Cobb Industrial Dr

Marietta

(800) 783-4591

Cobb Energy

1 reviews

1000 Emc Pky Ne

Marietta

(770) 429-2222

Other sources of info

====================

https://www.facebook.com/photo.php?fbid=267772576722222&set=a.267773076722172.1073741828.265434926955987&type=1&relevant_count=1

Also see full list here

http://emergency20wiki.org/wiki/index.php/Georgia_emergency_agencies_using_social_media

Or Crisis Whisperer list here

https://www.facebook.com/photo.php?fbid=267772576722222&set=a.267773076722172.1073741828.265434926955987&type=1&relevant_count=1

Here is the page of rss feeds related to emergency mgt in GA

http://output29.rssinclude.com/output?type=fb&id=835708&hash=0b8f685707dd08ead13166fc73a500e4

Let's Be Prepared Next Time!

Put an Emergency kit in your car asap - there is snow expected next week and mid Feb!!

a shovel

windshield scraper and small broom

flashlight with extra batteries

battery powered radio

water

snack food including energy bars

raisins and mini candy bars

matches and small candles

extra hats, socks and mittens

First aid kit with pocket knife

Necessary medications

blankets or sleeping bag

tow chain or rope

road salt, sand, or cat litter for traction

booster cables

emergency flares and reflectors

fluorescent distress flag and whistle to attract attention

Cell phone adapter to plug into lighter


Please see further down page below for full details of how to pick up abandoned cars


The main group https://www.facebook.com/groups/snowedoutatlanta got too big to help people so please use all these other groups according to location


Please consider using South Atlanta group if you are in that area:


https://www.facebook.com/groups/413082885492699/


Please consider using the East Cobb one if you are in that area


https://www.facebook.com/groups/589920607758603/

Please consider using the North Atlanta one if you are in the North of Atlanta but not in the East Cobb Area

https://www.facebook.com/groups/1444363039127776/

For Acworth use

https://www.facebook.com/groups/564807276947716/

West Atlanta use

https://www.facebook.com/groups/207247732814789/

Roswell area use (run by Kat-y Royale not by me)

https://www.facebook.com/groups/575657735850242/

For Dialysis Users see

https://www.facebook.com/groups/snowedoutdialysis/

(though we have no affiliation, we also have no knowledge of dialysis so we trust this group to provide you with what you need)

If you know of additional resources, email breakingnews@ajc.com and we will add the information to this list.

Note that other groups have cropped up starting SnowedOut - they are nothing to do with

the official groups (started by Michelle Sollicito) above though they appear to be helping people too.

PLEASE PLEASE POST HELP ON OUR MAP

If you can, place your address on this map if you are offering shelter:

https://www.facebook.com/groups/397839673695382/permalink/398071427005540/?stream_ref=2

The rss feed page has input from the following sources:

RSS Feeds

==========

AJC alerts

http://www.ajc.com/.../ajc-auto-list-iphone-topnews/aFKq/

CDC alerts

http://www2c.cdc.gov/podcasts/createrss.asp?t=r&c=19

http://emergency.cdc.gov/rss/hurricanepsas.xml

GA Weather alerts

http://alerts.weather.gov/cap/ga.php?x=1

One minute weather update from GEMA

http://www.gema.ga.gov/rss_generator.nsf/rss?openagent...

GEMA Website Updates

http://www.gema.ga.gov/rss_generator.nsf/rss?openagent...

GDOT (511)

News and alerts

http://cdn.511ga.org/RSS/alerts.xml

http://cdn.511ga.org/RSS/incidents.xml

USGS Significant Earthquakes from the past hour

http://earthquake.usgs.gov/.../significant_hour.atom&_bc=1

USGS Mag 4.5+ Earthquakes past hour

http://earthquake.usgs.gov/.../v1.0/summary/4.5_hour.atom

River alerts from National Weather Service

http://water.weather.gov/ahps2/rss/alert/ga.rss


GetReady

http://ready.ga.gov/GetReady/feed/

http://www.ready.ga.gov/rss/feed/press-releases


Complaints

=======

If you do not like what someone posts or comments, do not like it and do not comment on it - then it will simply disappear off of the page. If you keep liking and commenting you are giving them what they want - ATTENTION!

You can flag posts that you think should be removed. When we are really busy we may not have time to remove posts and in some cases we may keep posts that are flagged even though you do not like them because they may add value to the conversation for some people.


Admins

=====

(Admin names go here)


Here is some of the *additional* info I added for SnowStorm 2, in which people needed different information – e.g. about power outages

PLEASE READ THIS FIRST!!

DO NOT TRAVEL TODAY EXCEPT IN CASE OF EXTREME EMERGENCY!!!

(this page will be constantly updated also - if you have something to add PM me)

If you have a life-threatening emergency first call 911. After that consider the resources below.

EMAS

====

Useful for help with shelters, fallen trees and medical emergencies

Cobb EMA

http://portal.cobbcountyga.gov/index.php?option=com_content&id=388&Itemid=258

Fulton EMA

http://www.fultoncountyga.gov/afcema

POWER OUTAGES

===========

GENERATORS - if you are using one, please read this!!

http://www.nsc.org/news_resources/Resources/Documents/Portable_Generator_Safety_Tips.pdf

Georgia Power - Ice Storm Tips (Also report an outage here)

===============================

http://georgiapower.com/in-your-community/storm-center/before/prepare-icestorm.cshtml

Report an outage (888) 891-0938

Txt based outage reporting/checking http://www.georgiapower.com/about/outage-alerts-video.cshtml

Useful info when preparing for outages

========================

http://www.myajc.com/news/news/the-dark-side-avoiding-power-outage-problems/ndKJJ/?icmp=ajc_internallink_invitationbox_apr2013_ajcstubtomyajcpremium

Report outages at Marietta Power and Water

============================

To report a non-emergency problem: call 770-794-5160

Power-related emergencies: 770-794-5160

Other Utilities in the Marietta area

====================

Marietta City Utilities Board

675 N Marietta Pky Ne

Marietta

(770) 794-5192

Cobb Electric Membership Cor...

1000 Emc Pky Ne

Marietta

(770) 429-2100

Marietta City Water Department

627 N Marietta Pky Ne, ?#?B?

Marietta

(770) 794-5230

Industrial Power & Components ...

1536 Cobb Industrial Dr

Marietta

(800) 783-4591


Cobb Energy

1 reviews

1000 Emc Pky Ne

Marietta

(770) 429-2222


Sawnee EMC

770-887-2363

www.sawnee.com/storm


To see where Power Outages are currently, click here for Georgia Power outages

http://www.myfoxatlanta.com/link/676630/live-map-moitor-power-outages


Click here for Marietta Power outages

http://www.mariettaga.gov/city/mpw/power/outages


Coweta EMC outages

http://outage.utility.org/OMSWebMap/Map/OMSWebMap.htm


Contact/Useful info

======================

Children's Health phone line (do NOT go out if your kids are sick, call this line)

Children's Healthcare of Atlanta (CHOA) Advice Line is 404-250-5437. The DIRECT LINE to the CHOA NURSES is 404-785-3100


Warming Centers,Shelters etc

Kasim Reed's list of shelters and warming stations appears to be the best

https://www.facebook.com/KasimReed/posts/10152232755489669?stream_ref=10

http://www.gema.ga.gov/content/forms/ShelterInformation.pdf

Useful info, up to date

http://www.wsbradio.com/news/news/atlanta-traffic/nC7qX/

Police Precincts open for stranded motorists

http://www.gema.ga.gov/content/forms/PolicePrecinctsOpenForStrandedMotorists.pdf

School Closing info http://www.wsbtv.com/school-closings/search/

511 - Current Road situation map with cameras

http://www.511ga.org/

GEMA

Website: http://www.gema.ga.gov

E-mail:pao@gema.ga.gov

Phone: (404) 635-7000 or1-(800)-TRY-GEMA (1-800-879 4362)

Marietta

Call 770-794-5334 and the Marietta Police Department will assist you.

Kennesaw

Call 770-422-2505 and the Kennesaw Police Department will assist you.

Atlanta Police Dept

(404) 614-6544

https://www.facebook.com/AtlantaPoliceDpt

www.Twitter.com/atlanta_police

Cobb County Govt

http://portal.cobbcountyga.gov/index.php

Cobb County Police

770) 499-3900

Cobb DOT

(770) 528-1600

http://portal.cobbcountyga.gov/index.php?option=com_content&id=599&Itemid=299

Get Ready

http://ready.ga.gov

Red Cross shelter finder

http://app.redcross.org/nss-app/

USGS

http://earthquake.usgs.gov

National Weather Service

https://www.weather.gov

City of Atlanta

http://www.atlantaga.gov

on Facebook

www.facebook.com/cityofatlanta

Atlanta Fire Rescue Dept

www.facebook.com/atlantafirerescue

Atlanta Airport

www.facebook.com/hartsfieldjackson

http://atlanta-airport.com/


Mayor Kasim Reed www.Twitter.com/kasimreed

# Appendix 3 Emergency Kit Information

**Debra Gibson**
Question: I want to put an emergency kit in my car. Please name some things that would have helped everyone. One thing I will do asap is make an address book.

Like · Comment · January 29 at 11:51pm

👍 Kat-y Royale, John N Nita Spindler and 48 others like this.

📄 2 shares

💬 View previous comments                                    100 of 125

 **Kristen Peck** I had sub zero sleeping bag, freeze dried food, boots , socks, extra coat, extra pants, solar cell phone charger, knife, hammer, gloves, jumper cables, ( and a Come along ).
January 30 at 12:16am · Like · 👍3

 **Katharine Luongo** You can not keep gas in a container in your car- it is very dangerous .
January 30 at 12:17am · Like · 👍7

 **Katharine Luongo** Thermal blankets, hand warmers, water, flares, protein bars
January 30 at 12:19am · Like · 👍3

 **Jacqueline Petty** Blanket, Traction for shoes, shelf stable snacks, bottles water, first aid, meds for a few days.
January 30 at 12:21am · Like · 👍2

 **Katharine Luongo** water proof boots !!
January 30 at 12:21am · Like · 👍1

 **Jesse Metcalf Green** http://www.dmv.org/how-to-guides /emergency-kit.php...-
January 30 at 12:24am · Like · 👍1

 **Amy Millhorn Leonard** Jumper cables. Hard candy. Extra gloves. Extra set of clothes. Small bag of toiletries. Swiss Army knife. Chains.
January 30 at 12:26am · Like · 👍2

 **Josh Farley** Blankets water flashlight batteries matches flairs granola bars,a good pocket knife. And more blankets Every single car should have atleast those things!! Think survivalist
January 30 at 12:38am · Like · 👍2

 **Kitty Pride** Water proof, slip resistant boots/shoes. Extra socks. and everything else people posted here lol
January 30 at 12:39am · Like · 👍1

 **Josh Farley** I'm from ny. These are things we always made sure we had..
January 30 at 12:39am · Like · 👍2

 **Kitty Pride** Even if snow only comes 2 days out of the year, you got to prepare. People can actually freeze to death. In MN there were at least 7-10 people who froze to death from being stranded in their car. people have debated with me all day about Atlanta and this is how they do things. But if they don't listen they gon' learn one day
January 30 at 12:44am · Like · 👍2

January 30 at 12:44am · Like · 2

 **Josh Farley** U ALWAYS prepare for the worst and hope for the best. But not having an emergency survival kit is just dumb. And lots of blankets can combat shock.. cold weather. Can be used to insulate. Georgian I hope u learned from this. ALWAYS BE PREPARED!
January 30 at 12:46am · Like · 4

 **Kristen Peck** I can say my at was packed with everything I needed to stay over night in my car. I was one of the lucky ones and found a place to sleep
January 30 at 12:52am · Like · 2

 **Jean Cathryn McRae** Leigh Davis posted a list here.
January 30 at 1:11am · Like · 1

 **JoEllen Chambliss** We had a ice storm in Fort Worth last December and I discovered golf shoes were excellent for walking on ice. 🙂
January 30 at 1:17am · Like · 6

 **Jessica IdreamNcolor Bell** a container for human waste, water, hand sanitizer, non-persihable food, medication, blankets, wipes, two pair of underwear, socks, travel toothbrush, non-persihable food, band aids, rubbing alchohol, a knitted cap, warm gloves, plastic bags, sanitary napkins, waterless soap, gronola, (a box of MRE's), vitamin C, flashlight, emergency flares, fix a flat.......
January 30 at 1:35am · Like · 8

 **Carrie Schodtler Clark** you should definitly have some of those emergency blankets, they look like aluminum and they are just a few bucks in walmart.
January 30 at 1:37am · Like · 4

 **Carrie Schodtler Clark** Also solar chargers and spare battery packs, for night time use, are super inexpensive on Amazon.com. we have some anker brand that we got for $20-$50 depending on the charging capabilities.
January 30 at 1:38am · Like · 1

 **Mandy Olson Murdock** Small things that come in handy, a box of gallon size ziptop bags. Can be used to cover shoes for walking in snow, human waste disposal, collecting snow, ect..
I'm from WI originally and every fall I would put a small bag with matches, the single serve cereal boxes, a box of Ziploc bag, and blanket, gloves, and hat. And usually a cheap bag of kitty litter.
January 30 at 1:41am · Like · 6

 **Missy Herren Young** Extra clothes if no ones mentioned it 🙂
January 30 at 1:43am · Like · 2

 **Kimberly Baker** http://www.amazon.com/dp/B007IS1ZX8/?tag=047-20
January 30 at 1:45am · Like · 2

 **Carrie Schodtler Clark** oooooh, and a box of those hot hands air activated warmers. They had them at Sams pretty cheap, don't know if they still do, but they would be a FANTASTIC addition, add that to a few emergency blankets, and at least you won't freeze....
January 30 at 1:54am · Like · 3

 **Heather Potts** I seen hot hands for $1 each at the dollar general the other day.
January 30 at 1:54am · Like · 3

**Kimberly Baker** http://www.amazon.com/dp/B007IS1ZX8
/?tag=047-20
January 30 at 1:45am · Like · 👍2

**Carrie Schodtler Clark** oooooh, and a box of those hot hands air
activated warmers. They had them at Sams pretty cheap, don't
know if they still do, but they would be a FANTASTIC addition, add
that to a few emergency blankets, and at least you won't freeze....
January 30 at 1:54am · Like · 👍3

**Heather Potts** I seen hot hands for $1 each at the dollar general
the other day.
January 30 at 1:54am · Like · 👍3

**Carrie Schodtler Clark** http://www.amazon.com/Opteka...
/dp/B005ZSVZRY/ref=sr_1_10...

Solar charger for $22, NOT BAD!!!
January 30 at 1:56am · Like · 👍1

**Carrie Schodtler Clark** I LOVE Amazon. Just saying. 10
emergency blankets for less than 8 bucks.!!!
http://www.amazon.com/.../B000GC.../ref=pd_ecc_rvi_cart_4...
January 30 at 1:59am · Like · 👍1

**Liz Lizzard** I have a special needs baby so I would pack an
emergency kit with some of her medical supplies like catheters,
gloves, diapers and wipes as well as the usual.
January 30 at 2:02am · Like · 👍4

**Janet Countryman** metal coffee can and candles. will provide heat
and light in case of emergency
January 30 at 2:03am · Like · 👍5

**Carrie Schodtler Clark** If you have babies you should have
formula and water.
January 30 at 2:04am · Like · 👍3

**Tida Lynn Miller** I keep a battery powered phone charger and
extra batteries, non perishables, winter gear, blanket, pack of waters.
I will be investing in tire chains after this. lol
January 30 at 2:05am · Like · 👍5

**Monique Dixon** Cat Litter provides traction.
January 30 at 2:18am · Like · 👍5

**Carrie Schodtler Clark** EVERYONE should have in their cell, bc we
will all have back up power sources in our cars now, a contact that
is labeled : ICE (in case of emergency) and then the numbers you want
called....
January 30 at 2:29am · Like · 👍3

**Carrie Schodtler Clark** for those who didn't read that screen shot
,it was pretty small, 3 days of any medications, especially vital ones!
January 30 at 2:34am · Like · 👍2

**Justin Parker** Kitty litter (a few bags)
Flashlight with extra batteries
Glowsticks (can be used if you need medical help they are easy for
people to see and get you help if you arent able to do it yourself, can
also be used for other things)
Hand warmers
A little bit of money or a prepaid card from like walmart. Load up about
$20-$30 on it or so. It will allow you to stop and get gas and some
snacks and waters if at all necessary.

January 30 at 2:34am · Like · 💬2

**Justin Parker** Kitty litter (a few bags)
Flashlight with extra batteries
Glowsticks (can be used if you need medical help they are easy for
people to see and get you help if you arent able to do it yourself, can
also be used for other things)
Hand warmers
A little bit of money or a prepaid card from like walmart. Load up about
$20-$30 on it or so. It will allow you to stop and get gas and some
snacks and waters if at all necessary.

All this stuff is pretty cheap. I know for a fact that the litter at walmart is
$3 for a 20lb bag of clay litter i carry 2 of them at all times. Glowsticks
are very cheap too
January 30 at 2:45am · Like · 👍7

**Jennie Jane Hargrove** Candle with matches. It provides enough
heat to keep your hands/face warm. Candy bars. Those little
self-heating hand warmers you bust open. Blankets. Flares. Socks.
Mittens. Hat.
January 30 at 2:47am · Like · 👍4

**Michael Jackson** Road flares, kitty litter, Bottled water, energy bars,
a bright blanket or other signaling device for use during daylight,
blankets for warmth. Flashlight and a book to read.
January 30 at 3:02am · Like · 👍3

**Chris Lawrence Holley** jumper cables
January 30 at 3:07am · Like · 👍2

**Bonnie Evans** Blanket, heavy socks, hat, gloves, water, Protein
bars, flashlight.
January 30 at 3:12am · Like · 👍3

**Jacqui Smyth** Don't forget kitty litter....if you can't get enough
traction to get your car moving and all you cam do is doin your
tires, a sprinkle of kitty litter in front of your wheel tires will get you out
without having to fight with snow chains or leaving anything behind.
Also, sandwhich baggies and rubberbands. When I lived in
Pennsylvania and the snow was bad and we walked to the bus stop,
my mom used to that to us and we hated it. But, keeping your feet dry
is actually incredibly important, especially for those who get stranded
and have to walk in the snow! Weird, I know...but, it works!
January 30 at 3:15am · Like · 👍5

**Shelly Kosloski** I agree Michael Jackson. Road flares can be life
saving. And ALWAYS make sure your tailpipe is free of anything!
Dirt, weeds, snow! Could save your life. Also warm socks. If your
current socks get wet, you're screwed!
January 30 at 3:51am · Like · 👍5

**Cathy Roberts Brown** .
January 30 at 4:21am · Like

**Derek Townsend** Everbody that is giving here stuff for the cold is
stupid. All u need to is have COMMON-SENSE. So for what u need
in your car. The things u NEED are jumper cables, gas can, flash light,
small 24 piece ratchet set, cellphone charger, blanket (fire and for cold),
full size spare rim/tire, a good jack and 4 way lug tool. Ands that's
about it. Get stuff u know you need for u personaly. All that crazy crap
people sayin is nuts. Really people get a grip. AND EVERYONE GO GET
SNOW CHAINS FOR YOUR TIRES. Keep them at home and out away f

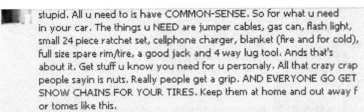

stupid. All u need to is have COMMON-SENSE. So for what u need in your car. The things u NEED are jumper cables, gas can, flash light, small 24 piece ratchet set, cellphone charger, blanket (fire and for cold), full size spare rim/tire, a good jack and 4 way lug tool. Ands that's about it. Get stuff u know you need for u personaly. All that crazy crap people sayin is nuts. Really people get a grip. AND EVERYONE GO GET SNOW CHAINS FOR YOUR TIRES. Keep them at home and out away f or tomes like this.

January 30 at 12:52pm · Edited · Like

**Derek Townsend** And for those that don't know how to put snow chains in your car you do it before u get stuck. And read the instructions.

January 30 at 4:28am · Like · 👍1

**Lisa Hall Head** Get the hand and feet warmers from Walmart for sure. And one of these. http://www.criticaltool.com/all-weather-emergency-blanket...

January 30 at 4:30am · Like · 👍2

**Amy Barnes** Kitty litter and rock salt - I used it to help clear out a piece of South Cobb Drive. And it works.

January 30 at 4:30am · Like · 👍4

**Ashmurr Moran** A foil heat blanket!!!!!!

January 30 at 4:30am · Like · 👍3

**Amy Barnes** Lotion as your hands can get really dry in the cold, too. And snack food such as canned tuna or protein shakes / bars.

January 30 at 4:31am · Like · 👍1

**Justin Parker** 📌Derek Townsend, wait til you need one of those items and it was be crap or so stupid as you put it. Everything I keep in my car has been used at one time or another. Any of this stuff can be used at any time for any reason. If you break down and have a bottle of water it will help especially if you are in this GA heat.

The jack and spare are in mostly every car and what good is a ratchet set if you dont know what you are doing? And think, if you had all that stuff with you last night would you have been comfortable? I mean since you have a ratchet set and a spare you wouldn't be hungry? Thirsty? Cold?

January 30 at 4:33am · Like · 👍7

**Lisa Hall Head** http://www.amazon.com/AAA-Piece-Explorer... /dp/B0006MQJ20

January 30 at 4:33am · Like · 👍2

**Amy Barnes** Bottled fluids - Starbucks coffee - as in the bottled frapucchinos or whatever they are - they're awesome to have as it gives a quick mental boost if you've stayed up a long time.

January 30 at 4:33am · Like · 👍2

**Lorie Firecracker McGinnis** Also, there is an item sold on QVC called a Helio. You can carry them in your purse to charge your phone so If you run out of gas and can't charge your cell phone or if you have to abandon your car, you'll have a way to keep your phone charged. Maybe even buy 2

January 30 at 4:33am · Like · 👍1

**Amy Barnes** And duct tape. Heeey - I wonder if we could have made duct tape "rope" for tires???

January 30 at 4:34am · Like · 👍1

**Lorie Firecracker McGinnis** Helio or Halo. I'm not sure

January 30 at 4:34am · Like · 👍1

**Justin Parker** These items are necessities for emergency situations. Not just if you get a flat or your battery is dead. That stuff is common sense. The other stuff that is mentioned helped me in a few bad situations. Cat litter helps with ice but it also helps if yo... See More
January 30 at 4:37am · Like · 👍3

**John N Nita Spindler** Debra Gibson -If you get stuck and *do not* have cat litter I've used my car mats (which most people have in their car) to get unstuck when I lived up north!! http://lifehacker.com/use-your-cars-floor-mats-to-escape...
January 30 at 4:44am · Like · 👍10

**Lorie Firecracker McGinnis** Great idea on the car mats!!!
January 30 at 4:51am · Like · 👍4

**Carolyn Aidman** Candles a can and lighters. One candle inside a car can raise the temperature 15°, could be life-saving.
January 30 at 4:57am · Like · 👍6

**Amy Barnes** Some moist food is essential because of dehydration.
January 30 at 4:58am · Like · 👍1

**Shirley Murphy-Taylor** keep sterno kits... I saw people telling others to eat snow, THAT IS THE WORST thing someone can do! It brings down your core body temp and hastens hypothermia!! Hand warmers, the foil blankets you (space blanket) get at walmart for about $2.00, beef j... See More
January 30 at 5:12am · Like · 👍8

**Sabrina de Man** Bottled Water, an extra phone charger, a zip lock bag with: TP, hand sanitizer, tissues. Protein bars or trail mix, a flashlight w/working batteries, jumper cables and a small first aid kit 😊
January 30 at 5:32am · Like · 👍9

**Jessica IdreamNcolor Bell** 🔵Derek Townsend, good for you, here's your gold star....If you have all the answers, and you are beyond community sharing of information, then why did you join this group, and if you have chains on your tires----- if all of the eight lanes are blocked w... See More
January 30 at 7:31am · Edited · Like · 👍7

**Jennifer Nguyen** Thermal blankets
January 30 at 7:21am · Like · 👍2

**Jennifer Eades Myerscough** A votive candle or other small candle, housed in an empty tin can can heat your car for hours. Make sure you crack the window a bit for fresh oxygen... make sure you also have matches to light it.

Cat litter can give your tires just enough traction to get off ice. A small shovel (you can get some that fold up small).... See More
January 30 at 7:25am · Like · 👍3

**Adair Rains Flowers** Glo-sticks
January 30 at 7:31am · Like · 👍2

**Anna Santillan** Even better than kitty litter, and cheaper might I add is the stuff you clean up oil spills & stuff with..the specific brand walmart carries is called oil-dri and is $4.22 for a 25lb bag. You can find it in the automotive section
January 30 at 8:01am · Like · 👍5

**Anna Santillan** Also in a camping or outdoors stores, you could buy some of those meals, they have a shelf life of a couple years. Similar to MRE's that Soldier's eat.
January 30 at 8:03am · Like · 👍2

---